# THE TABERNACLE:
# CAMPING WITH GOD

# THE TABERNACLE:

# Camping with GOD

### *by*
### STEPHEN F. OLFORD

## LOIZEAUX BROTHERS

**B. McCALL BARBOUR**
28 GEORGE IV BRIDGE
EDINBURGH EHI IES, SCOTLAND

FIRST EDITION, NOVEMBER 1971
SIXTH PRINTING, SEPTEMBER 1983

ISBN O-87213-675-2

*Library of Congress Catalog Card Number:* 78-173686

PRINTED IN THE UNITED STATES OF AMERICA

Dedicated

To the memory of my beloved father

FREDERICK ERNEST SAMUEL OLFORD

from whose notes and talks I learned so much about

CAMPING WITH GOD

# CONTENTS

# FOREWORD

The title of this book takes me back to my boyhood days in Angola, Portuguese West Africa, where as the son of missionary parents I knew what it was to trek and camp for weeks on end — as new areas were opened to the glorious light of the gospel. During those days of travel I recall how my father would lead family worship at dawn and then conduct a Bible study at dusk. Some of the deepest impressions I have carried throughout my subsequent life were made during those hours of ministry from God's Word. One particular series that I have never forgotten was on *the Tabernacle in the wilderness.* I can still visualize the scene as we sat, with African carriers, around the campfire immediately outside of our tent, listening with rapt attention to the expositions of divine truth. The "missionary's tent" served to represent the presence of God, while the fire symbolized the glory of God — as the Scriptures were unfolded and applied by the Holy Spirit. Those were sacred moments as I look back upon them; indeed, they were an experience of *camping with God.* I could never, therefore, think of the Tabernacle without relating it to that scene in the bush, with the central tent, the fire, and the silent worshipers.

Surely this is how the children of Israel must have thought of the Tabernacle, for in that "tent" God came down to camp with His people. In this way those Hebrews discovered that it is in the very nature of Deity to reveal Himself; and that the method of self-disclosure was to "tabernacle" with men.

In a sense, this is the essential message of the Bible. When we read, for instance, the first five books of Moses (Genesis to Deuteronomy) we trace the story of God's visits *to* men, culminating in God's camping *with* men in a Tabernacle so designed and constructed as to manifest the purpose, power, and Shekinah of the Divine Presence.

The New Testament opens in a similar manner, for the first five books are likewise concerned with the subject of camping with God. We read that "In the beginning was the Word, and the Word was with God, and the Word was God. . . . And the Word [became] flesh, and [tabernacled] among us, (and we beheld His glory, the glory as of the only begotten of the Father,) full of grace and truth" (John 1:1,14). As we move on from the four Gospels to the Acts of the Apostles we see that same grace and glory communicated to the early disciples until the outside world "took knowledge of them, that they had been with Jesus" (Acts 4:13).

The fact is that God created man for fellowship, and He will never be satisfied until that fellowship is realized to the full — not only here on earth, but throughout the ages of eternity (1 John 1:1-10).

So as we come to the study of the Tabernacle, we shall learn that the "tent of testimony" expressed two facts in the religious life of the children of Israel. In the first place, it represented the presence of God among His people, standing as it did in the center of the camp. In the second place, it typified the divinely appointed means by which sinful man could approach God, who was otherwise unapproachable because of His unspeakable holiness and ineffable majesty.

It is my earnest prayer that as these chapters are studied the Holy Spirit will give each reader a genuine experience of *camping with God.* In sharing this burden, however, I am obliged to point out that a volume on the Tabernacle is nothing new! Others have written exhaustively on this subject, as the bibliography contained in this book reveals. It is hoped, nevertheless, that similar expositions under different headings and with renewed emphasis will bring home to each reader what is the supreme message of the Tabernacle. Of course, this message is *Christ*, as He so clearly stated to those two disciples on the Emmaus road when, "beginning at Moses and all the prophets, He expounded unto them in all the scriptures the things concerning Himself" (Luke 24:27). God grant that as we read, learn, and inwardly digest these "things concerning Himself" we shall be able to say, "Did not our heart burn within us, while He talked with us by the way, and while He opened to us the scriptures?" (Luke 24:32)

Finally, I wish to express a deep debt of gratitude to my father, now in glory, who first introduced me to the teaching of the Tabernacle; also to other expositors who have shaped my thinking throughout the years; and to the authors of the works from which I have drawn heavily. Likewise, I want to thank John Phillips, director of the Correspondence School, Emmaus Bible School, Oak Park, Illinois, who spurred me on to publish these studies; and to those who have looked through these chapters and have offered valuable suggestions. Last, but not least, I desire to record my appreciation to Miss Victoria Kuhl who has patiently and prayerfully typed the manuscript for publication.

All this "labor of love" will have been more than worth while if those who peruse these pages learn the privilege, the pleasure, and the power that come through camping with God.

Stephen F. Olford
*Calvary Baptist Church*
*New York City*

# Chapter 1

# THE INTRODUCTION

## *Scriptures for Study*

And the LORD spake unto Moses, saying, Speak unto the children of Israel, that they bring Me an offering: of every man that giveth it willingly with his heart ye shall take My offering. And this is the offering which ye shall take of them; gold, and silver, and brass, And blue, and purple, and scarlet, and fine linen, and goats' hair, And rams' skins dyed red, and badgers' skins, and shittim wood, Oil for the light, spices for anointing oil, and for sweet incense, Onyx stones, and stones to be set in the ephod, and in the breastplate. And let them make Me a sanctuary; that I may dwell among them. According to all that I show thee, after the pattern of the tabernacle, and the pattern of all the instruments thereof, even so shall ye make it (Exodus 25:1-9).

Now of the things which we have spoken this is the sum: We have such an high priest, who is set on the right hand of the throne of the Majesty in the heavens; A minister of the sanctuary, and of the true tabernacle, which the Lord pitched, and not man. For every high priest is ordained to offer gifts and sacrifices: wherefore it is of necessity that this man have somewhat also to offer. For if He were on earth, He should not be a priest, seeing that there are priests that offer gifts according to the law: Who serve unto the example and shadow of heavenly things, as Moses was admonished of God when he was about to make the tabernacle: for, See, saith He, that thou make all things according to the pattern showed to thee in the mount (Hebrews 8:1-5).

13

## THE INTRODUCTION

Scriptures for Study: Exodus 25:1-9; Hebrews 8:1-5

### I. THE SETTING OF THE TABERNACLE

1. The Period

2. The Place

### II. THE SYMBOLISM OF THE TABERNACLE

1. The Materials of the Tabernacle
   a. Metals
   b. Colors
   c. Fabrics
   d. Wood
   e. Oil
   f. Spices
   g. Stones

2. The Measures of the Tabernacle
   a. Number Three
   b. Number Four
   c. Number Five
   d. Number Seven
   e. Number Twelve
   f. Number Forty

### III. THE SIGNIFICANCE OF THE TABERNACLE

1. The Mentions of the Tabernacle

2. The Ministry of the Tabernacle
   a. The Christ
   b. The Church
   c. The Christian

3. The Message of the Tabernacle
   a. The Way of Introduction — the gate of the outer court
   b. The Way of Reconciliation — the brazen altar
   c. The Way of Separation — the laver
   d. The Way of Illumination — the golden candlestick
   e. The Way of Satisfaction — the table of showbread
   f. The Way of Intercession — the altar of incense
   g. The Way of Communion — the ark of the covenant

The Tabernacle was an object lesson to the children of Israel for nearly five hundred years, from Moses to David. It gave place to the Temple, the more permanent structure, during the reign of Solomon. Although the Tabernacle itself has long since ceased to exist, its lessons remain to this day. Indeed, as Dr. M. R. DeHaan has pointed out, "There is no portion of Scripture richer in meaning, or more perfect in its teaching of the plan of redemption, than this divinely designed building." So as we anticipate the studies before us, we can be assured of "a feast of good things"!

To help us understand what is to follow in our examination of the Tabernacle, it is necessary in this introductory chapter to consider:

## I. THE SETTING OF THE TABERNACLE

This has to do primarily with the period and the place of its appearance.

1. The Period

"And the LORD spake unto Moses, saying, Speak unto the children of Israel, that they . . . make Me a sanctuary; that I may dwell among them" (Exodus 25:1-2,8).

These ancient pilgrims had become a redeemed people. God could never dwell on earth with His people until the Red Sea was crossed; or, in other words, until redemption was accomplished. He visited Adam in the Garden, appeared to and communicated with the patriarchs, but until He had redeemed His people out of Egypt nothing is said of making a sanctuary in which He might dwell. The Tabernacle was the proof of redemption effected by purchase and power. Not only had the children of Israel been sheltered under the blood, but they had been brought through the Red Sea with the right hand of power. In this way God had brought a redeemed people into fellowship with Himself, He being the One around whom they were gathered.

Such is always God's thought in redemption. He does not only save men and women, He sanctifies them, or sets them apart as a people capable of worship and witness. While the children of Israel were in Egypt, they could neither worship nor witness, for they were inescapable slaves and idolatrous sinners. This is why God, through Moses, had to say to Pharaoh again and again, "Let My people go, that they may serve Me" (Exodus 8:1,20; 9:1; etc.).

2. The Place

The Tabernacle was not erected in Egypt, nor primarily in Canaan, but in the wilderness. This is a point of some importance. As we have just seen, Egypt was a land of idolatry (Ezekiel 20:5-9), and therefore no place for a sanctuary for God. Neither was the Tabernacle to be built in Canaan. It is true that it was stationed in Shiloh for some time, but remained in Canaan only until Solomon's Temple was completed (Joshua 18:1; 1 Chronicles 16:39).

The Tabernacle was essentially for pilgrims in the desert, with Egypt behind them and Canaan before them. Therefore, such lessons as the Tabernacle would teach us are related essentially to our pilgrim life, as we make our way beyond Canaan to Heaven itself.

As we shall see in later studies, the Tabernacle, while in the wilderness, was always pitched on the sand. With all its rich furnishings and ornate decorations no provision was ever made to cover the sand. The contact of the priest's feet with the sand was ever a reminder that they were on a journey and had not reached their final destination. Those of us who understand the deeper lesson in this can never be so heavenly minded that we are of no earthly use.

## II. THE SYMBOLISM OF THE TABERNACLE

The study of symbology throughout the Old Testament is fascinating. Particularly is this so in connection with the Tabernacle. What we have to watch is the extremes to which expositors of the Scripture tend to go. There are those who see very little significance in the symbolism of the Bible. This of course is without any scriptural warrant, for the Bible itself interprets its own symbology. Then again there are others who press the symbolism to such lengths as to warp all true interpretation. What we need is the balance of the Holy Spirit, whose ministry is to "guide . . . into all truth" (or truth without error, John 16:13). The writer to the Hebrews is our best example of balanced interpretation, as we shall see in future studies. One of his key phrases is "the Holy Ghost . . . signifying" (Hebrews 9:8).

The symbolism with which we shall be concerned has to do with:

1. The Materials of the Tabernacle

These include metals, colors, fabrics, wood, oil, spices, and stones (see Exodus 25:3-7). In considering the typical import of these materials, we must, as I have inferred above, avoid dogmatism. On the other hand, it is generally accepted that the spiritual significations of the materials employed are as follows:

a. *Metals. Gold* typifies the deity of our Lord Jesus Christ (Revelation 3:18), and also divine righteousness, as seen in the mercy seat (Exodus 25:17). *Silver* typifies redemption, as seen in the atonement money (Exodus 30:12-16; Numbers 18:16). *Brass* typifies the death of Christ, as meeting man's responsibility toward God, as seen in the brazen altar (Exodus 27:3; Revelation 1:15).

b. *Colors.* The main colors are blue, purple, and scarlet, which occur in this combination and order about twenty-eight times in the book of Exodus.

*Blue,* the heavenly color, typifies Christ as the *spiritual* One, or heavenly Man (1 Corinthians 15:47-48; John 1:18). He was "holy, harmless, undefiled, separate from sinners, and made higher than the heavens" (Hebrews 7:26).

*Purple* typifies Christ as the sovereign One, the "KING OF KINGS AND LORD OF LORDS," who will reign universally (Revelation 19:16). Before His crucifixion, you will remember that even in mockery "they clothed Him with purple, and platted a crown of thorns, and put it about His head, And began to salute Him, Hail, King of the Jews!" (Mark 15:17-18)

*Scarlet* typifies Christ as the *sacrificial* One. This sacrificial color embodies the entire thought of redemption. The song of the redeemed is: "Thou art worthy . . . for Thou wast slain, and hast redeemed us to God by Thy blood out of every kindred, and tongue, and people, and nation; And hast made us unto our God kings and priests" (Revelation 5:9-10; see also Numbers 19:6; Leviticus 14:4; Hebrews 9:11-14, 19,23,28).

c. *Fabrics. Fine linen* speaks of *righteousness* (Revelation 19:8). This righteousness, of course, is the imputed righteousness of Christ. "But of Him are ye in Christ Jesus, who of God is made unto us wisdom, and righteousness, and sanctification, and redemption" (1 Corinthians 1:30).

*Goats' hair* speaks of *serviceableness*. Garments of goats' hair were worn by the prophets (see Zechariah 13:4-5). So the thought is of serviceableness in the prophetic office.

*Rams' skins,* dyed red, speak of *devotedness* in the priestly office. The breast of the ram was waved before the Lord for the consecration of Aaron (see Exodus 29:26-27).

*Badgers' skins* speak of *holiness,* repelling every form of evil (see Hebrews 7:26). These skins also illustrate the natural man's view of Christ, having "no form nor comeliness" (Isaiah 53:2).

d. *Wood.* The only wood referred to in the construction of the Tabernacle is the *shittim* or *acacia* wood. Shittim wood speaks of the incorruptibility of the human nature of our Lord. In Him there was no taint, corruption, or sin. Luke says of Him: "That holy thing which shall be born of thee shall be called the Son of God" (1:35; see also Acts 2:31).

It is interesting to observe here that there were four kinds of wood specified for Solomon's Temple, namely, cedar, fir, algum, and olive. In Ezekiel's Temple the palm tree was used, emblematic of rest and victory.

e. *Oil.* Oil typifies God's Holy Spirit, who is called in the New Testament "the anointing" (1 John 2:27). Kings, prophets, and priests were anointed with oil in Old Testament times.

f. *Spices.* These typify the fragrance of Christ before God (2 Corinthians 2:14-15).

g. *Stones.* Onyx and precious stones typify the preciousness of believers to God as seen in Christ (Malachi 3:17).

2. The Measures of the Tabernacle

As we proceed in these studies, we shall be impressed again and again with certain recurring numbers. Their very repetition and association symbolize certain precious truths; for example:

a. *Number Three.* This speaks of abundant testimony (see Matthew 18:16). So we have the testimony of God the Father, God the Son, and God the Holy Spirit.

This abundant testimony is illustrated in numerous "threes" throughout the whole construction of the Tabernacle, such as three sections composing the Tabernacle: the holiest of all, the holy place, and the court; three metals in the construction: gold, silver, and brass; three liquids employed in the service of the Tabernacle: blood, water, and oil; three colors used in the curtains: blue, purple, and scarlet; three types of sacrifices offered of the herd, e.g., bullocks; of the flock, e.g., sheep or goats; of the fowls, e.g., turtledoves or young pigeons; and so on.

b. *Number Four.* Four speaks of what is universal or world-wide. We talk about the "four winds" (Ezekiel 37:9), or "the four corners of the earth" (Isaiah 11:12). Look for the four coverings of the Tabernacle. There is the foursquare brazen altar, the four horns of the altar. There are four pillars upholding the hanging gate of the outer court, and then there are the four spices in the holy anointing oil (Exodus 30:23-25).

c. *Number Five,* and its multiples. Most scholars accept five as speaking of human responsibility. In its multiples it only intensifies the thought. It is the figure which is stamped on the human frame — five fingers, denoting human responsibility in work; five toes, denoting human responsibility in walk; five senses, denoting human responsibility in receptiveness. Five is also understood to signify the grace of God, e.g., the provision of grace (Matthew 14:17; 16:9), and the forgiveness of grace (Luke 7:41-42).

d. *Number Seven.* Since six is the number which denotes the height of human attainment, it must be ever short of perfection. Seven speaks of divine perfection. Seven was the number of the golden candlesticks. Seven was the number of items that went to furnish the Tabernacle, i.e., the ark, mercy seat, showbread, golden candlestick, brazen altar, brazen laver, and golden altar of incense.

e. *Number Twelve.* Twelve speaks of administration. Twelve is the number of the months of the year, setting forth God's administration in nature. Twelve is the number of the tribes of Israel, setting forth God's administration in government on behalf of His earthly people. Twelve is the number of loaves on the showbread table, setting forth God's administration in the support and maintenance of His people. Twelve was the number of precious stones on the breastplate of the high priest, setting forth our Lord's administration in love and representation of His people in the presence of God.

f. *Number Forty.* Forty is the compound of ten times four, and speaks of the full measure of man's responsibility Godward and manward. It sets forth the full measure of probation and testing. Forty years marked the length of the wilderness journey of the children of Israel.

Much more might be said on the symbology of Bible numbers, but this must suffice to illustrate the kind of thing we must look for in our study of the Tabernacle.

## III. THE SIGNIFICANCE OF THE TABERNACLE

In seeking to interpret the Tabernacle, we must not dogmatize but humbly follow the method of the Holy Spirit as illustrated in the Epistle to the Hebrews. Referring there to the Tabernacle and the priesthood, He speaks of the "shadow of heavenly things" (Hebrews 8:5); "the patterns of things in the heavens" (Hebrews 9:23); "the figures of the true" (Hebrews 9:24); "a shadow of good things to come" (Hebrews 10:1). Thus it is clear that the Tabernacle was intended to signify spiritual realities. In other words, in the Tabernacle we see shadows, patterns, and figures of heavenly or spiritual things that are revealed in Christ. This may be gathered from the significance of:

1. The Mentions of the Tabernacle

It is most remarkable to discover that no less than fifty chapters in the Old and New Testaments are devoted to the construction, ritual, and priesthood of the Tabernacle and the meaning of them all. There are thirteen in Exodus, eighteen in Leviticus, thirteen in Numbers, and two in Deuteronomy; then four in Hebrews. The significance of this fact is all the more apparent when we remember that the whole story of creation takes up only two chapters of the book of Genesis.

2. The Ministry of the Tabernacle

In a very unique way, the Tabernacle illustrates the ministry of:

a. *The Christ.* To the anointed eye, every detail of the Tabernacle points to some aspect of the Person and work of our Saviour. John tells us that "the Word became flesh, and [tabernacled] among us (and we beheld His glory, glory as of the only begotten from the Father), full of grace and truth" (John 1:14, R.V.). Just as the Tabernacle in the wilderness was the actual visible dwelling place of God in all His Shekinah glory, so in Christ dwells all the fullness of the Godhead bodily (Colossians 2:9). We shall revel in discovering in every detail of the Tabernacle, from the smallest pin to the large pieces of furniture, aspects of the Person and work of Christ (see Luke 24:27).

b. *The Church.* There are those who tell us that the Church is not directly referred to in the Old Testament, since it is a mystery hidden in all ages and revealed by the Holy Spirit in New Testament times (Ephesians 3:1-21; 5:23-33; Colossians 1:20-29). On the other hand, no one can read the Old Testament, and particularly study the Tabernacle, without seeing illustrative mentions of the Church.

When Paul speaks of the people of God being "builded together for an habitation of God through the Spirit" (Ephesians 2:22), he is describing just what the Tabernacle represented. The ministry of the Church is that of worship and witness, and we shall see in later studies just how that was the function of the Tabernacle.

c. *The Christian.* The Tabernacle is also a type of the Christian. The believer in Christ is the dwelling place of God. We read of "Christ in [us,] the hope of glory" (Colossians 1:27). Again: "Your life is hid with Christ in God" (Colossians 3:3). Paul talks of our bodies as being the temple of the Holy Spirit who dwelleth in us (1 Corinthians 3:16).

In a remarkable way, the entire person of the Christian represents the three compartments of the Tabernacle. The body corresponds to the outer court: it is the outer and visible part of our personality; it is the place of sacrifice and cleansing (see Romans 12:1-2; 1 John 1:7,9). The soul answers to the holy place, and therefore is that aspect of our personality which worships and enjoys fellowship with other believers, eating at the table, walking in the light, and interceding in prayer. The spirit speaks of the believer's inner holy of holies — the deepest hidden life, the individual and personal communion of one sheltered under the blood (John 4:23; Romans 1:9); it is the place of spiritual victory. As such, the Tabernacle speaks of the whole ministry of the New Testament Christian.

3. The Message of the Tabernacle

This can be summed up in a twofold proposition:

God's appearance to man in grace.

Man's approach to God in faith.

It is of very great significance that in giving the instructions for the construction of the Tabernacle, God begins with the ark and concludes with the brazen altar; whereas in the use of the Tabernacle, man commences with the brazen altar and moves through to the holy of holies and the ark of the covenant. That is the Christian gospel.

Christianity is unique in that it is the only religion which claims that God has taken the initiative in revealing Himself to man. All other religions describe man's search after God. But having revealed Himself to man by leaving His throne and humbling Himself unto death — even the death of the cross — God has effected a plan of salvation for man to approach Him by faith. That simple way of salvation is beautifully illustrated in seven steps, which we shall consider in more detail later.

For the present, let us note that for the penitent sinner who comes by faith there is:

a. *The Way of Introduction* — The gate of the outer court. Jesus said: "Enter ye in at the strait gate . . . because strait is the gate, and narrow is the way, which leadeth unto life" (Matthew 7:13-14).

b. *The Way of Reconciliation* — the brazen altar. "God was in Christ, reconciling the world unto Himself. . . . For He hath made Him to be sin for us, who knew no sin; that we might be made the righteousness of God in Him" (2 Corinthians 5:19,21).

c. *The Way of Separation* — the laver. Speaking to His disciples Jesus said: "He that is washed needeth not save to wash his feet, but is clean every whit" (John 13:10). Later He said: "Now ye are clean through the word which I have spoken unto you" (John 15:3).

d. *The Way of Illumination* — the golden candlestick. Jesus said: "I am the light of the world: he that followeth Me shall not walk in darkness, but shall have the light of life" (John 8:12).

e. *The Way of Satisfaction* — the table of showbread. Jesus said: "I am the bread of life: he that cometh to Me shall never hunger; and he that believeth on Me shall never thirst" (John 6:35).

f. *The Way of Intercession* — the altar of incense. "By Him therefore let us offer the sacrifice of praise to God continually, that is, the fruit of our lips giving thanks to His name" (Hebrews 13:15).

g. *The Way of Communion* — the ark of the covenant. "Truly our fellowship is with the Father, and with His Son Jesus Christ" (1 John 1:3).

So I have tried, in this introductory chapter, to bring such background information and instruction as will help us to study more intelligently, and enjoy more fully, the precious truths that are embodied in the setting, symbolism, and significance of the Tabernacle. May the Lord Jesus become increasingly precious to us as we search for Him and find Him in the variegated glories of this Old Testament picture.

# Chapter 2

## THE PURPOSE

### *Scriptures for Study*

And the LORD spake unto Moses, saying, Speak unto the children of Israel, that they bring Me an offering: of every man that giveth it willingly with his heart ye shall take My offering. And this is the offering which ye shall take of them; gold, and silver, and brass, and blue, and purple, and scarlet, and fine linen, and goats' hair, and rams' skins dyed red, and badgers' skins, and shittim wood, Oil for the light, spices for anointing oil, and for sweet incense, Onyx stones, and stones to be set in the ephod, and in the breastplate. And let them make Me a sanctuary; that I may dwell among them. According to all that I show thee, after the pattern of the tabernacle, and the pattern of all the instruments thereof, even so shall ye make it (Exodus 25:1-9).

The one lamb thou shalt offer in the morning; and the other lamb thou shalt offer at even: And with the one lamb a tenth deal of flour mingled with the fourth part of an hin of beaten oil; and the fourth part of an hin of wine for a drink offering. And the other lamb thou shalt offer at even, and shalt do thereto according to the meat offering of the morning, and according to the drink offering thereof, for a sweet savour, an offering made by fire unto the LORD. This shall be a continual burnt offering throughout your generations at the door of the tabernacle of the congregation before the LORD: where I will meet you, to speak there unto thee. And there I will meet with the children of Israel, and the tabernacle shall be sanctified by My glory. And I will sanctify the tabernacle of the congregation, and the altar: I will sanctify also both Aaron and his sons, to minister to Me in the priest's office. And I will dwell among the children of Israel, and will be their God. And they shall know that I am the LORD their God, that brought them forth out of the land of Egypt, that I may dwell among them: I am the LORD their God (Exodus 29:39-46).

Then verily the first covenant had also ordinances of divine service, and a worldly sanctuary. For there was a tabernacle made; the first, wherein was the candlestick, and the table, and the showbread; which is called the sanctuary. And after the second veil, the tabernacle which is called the Holiest of all; Which had the golden censer, and the ark of the covenant overlaid round about with gold, wherein was the golden pot that had manna, and Aaron's rod that budded, and the tables of the covenant; And over it the cherubims of glory shadowing the mercy seat; of which we cannot now speak particularly.

Now when these things were thus ordained, the priests went always into the first tabernacle, accomplishing the service of God. But into the second went the high priest alone once every year, not without blood, which he offered for himself, and for the errors of the people: The Holy Ghost this signifying, that the way into the holiest of all was not yet made manifest, while as the first tabernacle was yet standing: Which was a figure for the time then present, in which were offered both gifts and sacrifices, that could not make him that did the service perfect, as pertaining to the conscience; Which stood only in meats and drinks, and divers washings, and carnal ordinances, imposed on them until the time of reformation.

But Christ being come an high priest of good things to come, by a greater and more perfect tabernacle, not made with hands, that is to say, not of this building; Neither by the blood of goats and calves, but by His own blood He entered in once into the holy place, having obtained eternal redemption for us (Hebrews 9:1-12).

## THE PURPOSE

Scriptures for Study: Exodus 25:1-9; 29:39-46; Hebrews 9:1-12

### I. THE IMMEDIATE PURPOSE

1. A Place of Worship
   a. The Established Relationship
   b. The Experienced Revelation

2. A Place of Witness
   a. The Presence of God
   b. The Purity of God
   c. The Protection of God
   d. The Provision of God

### II. THE ULTIMATE PURPOSE

1. His Person

2. His Work

The Word of God makes it quite plain that there is a twofold purpose in the divine conception and human construction of the Tabernacle. There was first an immediate purpose, and then an ultimate purpose.

## I. THE IMMEDIATE PURPOSE

This was to wean the children of Israel from the base idolatry of Egypt and set before them a pure and noble ideal of worship and witness. The natural tendency of these ancient pilgrims was downward and backward, as can be well illustrated by their lapse into idolatry, when they worshiped the golden calf (Exodus 32). But in the worship of the unseen and unrepresented God a new era of religious history was ushered in, which in due course was to influence the whole world; for let us never forget that "salvation is of the Jews" (John 4:22). So the immediate purpose of the Tabernacle was the divine provision of:

1. A Place of Worship

When Jesus said to the woman of Samaria, "God is a Spirit: and they that worship Him must worship Him in spirit and in truth" (John 4:24), He was giving expression to a profound principle of worship. No one can worship God without an established relationship and an experienced revelation. True worship must be in spirit and in truth. The phrase "in spirit" presupposes an established relationship; "in truth" predicates an experienced revelation.

Now as we examine the Scriptures concerning the purpose of the Tabernacle, we find that this principle of worship is plainly evident:

a. *The Established Relationship.* God said: "Let them make Me a sanctuary; that I may dwell among them" (Exodus 25:8). And again: "I will dwell among the children of Israel, and will be their God" (Exodus 29:45). This was an entirely new relationship with men. Of old, Jehovah had walked in the Garden of Eden and had held intercourse with Adam; He had visited the patriarchs and communicated His will to them; but He had never had a home on earth until the Tabernacle was erected among His redeemed and separated people.

In a similar way, we can never worship until God dwells in us by the presence and power of the Holy Spirit (Ephesians 2:22). In his letter to the Philippians, the Apostle Paul reminds us that "we are the circumcision, which worship God in the spirit, and rejoice in Christ Jesus, and have no confidence in the flesh" (3:3).

b. *The Experienced Revelation.* God's word to His people was not only that He wanted to *dwell* among them, but also to *meet* with them. So we read: "This shall be a continual burnt offering throughout your generations at the door of the tabernacle of the congregation before the LORD: where I will meet you, to speak there unto thee. And there I will meet with the children of Israel, and the tabernacle shall be sanctified by My glory" (Exodus 29:42-43).

This meeting with Moses, Aaron, and the people was the way in which God revealed Himself to them. The very phrase "the tabernacle of the congregation" (Exodus 29:42) means "the tent of meeting." A congregation is a meeting of individuals for fellowship and counsel. Thus the Tabernacle was essentially a place where man met with God, and God with man. In a similar way today, we can only worship as God meets with us through the revelation of His Word, so that our response to Him is "in truth" as well as "in spirit."

The Tabernacle was the divine provision of a place of worship, and also:

2. A Place of Witness

Twice over in Numbers 17 this tent of meeting was called "the tabernacle of witness" (verses 7-8); and this is exactly what it was, both to the children of Israel and to the strangers without the camp. It witnessed to:

a. *The Presence of God.* As we shall be seeing in later studies, the record of the completion of the Tabernacle is an extremely thrilling one. After the words, "So Moses finished the work," we read, "Then a cloud covered the tent of the congregation, and the glory of the LORD filled the tabernacle" (Exodus 40:33-34). That cloud, thereafter, was the outward witness of the presence of God among His people. So long as it remained, the children of Israel could count upon the divine presence. "The cloud of the LORD was upon the tabernacle by day, and fire was on it by night, in the sight of all the house of Israel, throughout all their journeys" (Exodus 40:38).

b. *The Purity of God.* The root meaning of the word "tabernacle" or "sanctuary" carries the thought of holiness or sacredness, and therefore fitly describes not only the place, but the whole purpose of the Tabernacle. If you were to take a concordance and follow the word "holy," as related to the Tabernacle, in the book of Exodus alone you would find some thirty-one or more occurrences. The engraving on the plate of pure gold, attached to the miter and worn by Aaron, the high priest, sums up this witness to the purity of God. The words were to read "HOLINESS TO THE LORD" (Exodus 28:36). The whole Tabernacle was carefully guarded from anything that might defile or disturb the sanctity of God's dwelling place. The Levites were the jealous custodians of the sacred vessels and ministers of the sanctuary. Their tents flanked the outer court and their eyes were ever on the watch for the unauthorized intruder.

Then, of course, there was the curtained enclosure of fine twined linen which effectually precluded an outsider from witnessing what went on in the outer court. Thus the inside of the court and of the Tabernacle itself could neither be seen nor entered from outside. Everything was screened from public gaze and protected from unhallowed approach. There was no entrance save by the one door on the east. All this and more eloquently witnessed to the purity of God. The court was called "the holy place" (Leviticus 6:16,26): the first section of the Tabernacle "the holy place" (Exodus 26:33), and the second section "the most holy place" (Exodus 26:34). No wonder we are exhorted to be "holy in all manner of conversation; Because it is written, Be ye holy; for I am holy" (1 Peter 1:15-16).

c. *The Protection of God.* While that august pillar of cloud by day and fire by night stood over the Tabernacle nothing could touch the people of God. No force could approach their tents; no foe could stand against them. At night the Israelites had light to see; in the day they had shade from the heat of an almost tropical sun. "So it was alway: the cloud covered it by day, and the appearance of fire by night" (Numbers 9:16, see also verses 15-23).

The Psalmist sums up the witness to this protection when he says: "The LORD is thy keeper: the LORD is thy shade upon thy right hand. The sun shall not smite thee by day, nor the moon by night. The LORD shall preserve thee from all evil: He shall preserve thy soul" (Psalm 121:5-7).

d. *The Provision of God.* God is the reality behind all symbols. This wonderful fact is gloriously brought out in the Lord's promise to the exiles in Babylon, when He says, "I . . . will . . . be to [you] as a little sanctuary" (Ezekiel 11:16).

For all countries, classes, and conditions, and therefore all changing experiences of life, that promise holds good. All that the Tabernacle stood for was God's promise of provision for His people in the wilderness; and since then, for all His people down through the centuries. Whatever the children of Israel required was guaranteed to them, so long as the Tabernacle of witness stood.

So we see that the immediate purpose of the Tabernacle was the divine provision of a place of worship and witness.

## II. THE ULTIMATE PURPOSE

The ultimate purpose of the Tabernacle was to point to the coming of Him in whom all object lessons are fulfilled. Even the priests and Levites must have realized the imperfection and incompleteness of the Tabernacle with its associated ritual. As they carried out their duties of sacrifice and ceremony — daily, weekly, monthly, and yearly — they must have realized again and again that all this pointed on to something yet future. Today we know how true this is, as we read the Epistle to the Hebrews and see the Holy Spirit's interpretation of the meaning and ministry of that Tabernacle of old.

So the ultimate purpose of the Tabernacle was to prefigure Christ in:

1. His Person

Having touched upon the ritual of the Tabernacle of old, the writer to the Hebrews concludes by saying: "The Holy Ghost this signifying, that the way into the holiest of all was not yet made manifest. . . . But Christ being come an high priest of good things to come, by a greater and more perfect tabernacle, not made with hands, that is to say, not of this building; Neither by the blood of goats and calves, but by His own blood He entered in once into the holy place, having obtained eternal redemption for us" (Hebrews 9:8,11-12).

Christ is the *perfect Tabernacle.* In Him is fulfilled all that the Tabernacle in the wilderness typified and prefigured.

It is a point of great significance to observe that the two basic materials in the structure of the Tabernacle were *gold* and *wood.* The gold, of course, speaks of Christ's deity, while the wood typifies His humanity. The gold was of a refined quality, and therefore the most precious metal known to man. The shittim wood was of the acacia tree, which grew sparsely in the desert regions through which the children of Israel were traveling. The result of growth under the most adverse circumstances, it speaks of Christ as the "root out of a dry ground," and as the "tender plant" (Isaiah 53:2). It is also outwardly an unattractive tree, prefiguring Him of whom it was said: "He hath no form nor comeliness; and when we shall see Him, there is no beauty that we should desire Him" (Isaiah 53:2). The shittim wood is incorruptible, and so typifies the holy body of the Lord Jesus which saw no corruption, even when cut off in death (Acts 2:25-28).

Bringing these two great thoughts of the gold and wood together, we have the unique Person of our Lord Jesus Christ. John sums it up when he says: "The Word was made flesh, and dwelt [or tabernacled] among us, (and we beheld His glory, the glory as of the only begotten of the Father,) full of grace and truth" (John 1:14). The concept of these two perfect natures in one personality is a mystery which we cannot fathom, but which we can believe to our eternal good. Paul says: "And without controversy great is the mystery of godliness: God was manifest in the flesh" (1 Timothy 3:16).

The Redeemer must, of necessity, be both God and man, in order to mediate between God and men. "There is one God, and one mediator between God and men, the man Christ Jesus" (1 Timothy 2:5). Because God of very God, He undertakes for men; because Man of very man, He understands men. So we see how the Tabernacle speaks of the Person of Christ.

It also speaks of:

2. His Work

He is not only the perfect Tabernacle, He is the *perfect Priest.* The Spirit of God tells us that "Christ being come an high priest of good things to come . . . by His own blood . . . entered in once into the holy place, having obtained eternal redemption for us" (Hebrews 9:11-12). As perfect High Priest, He exercises the ministry of *introduction* at the door of the outer court, the ministry of *reconciliation* at the brazen altar, the ministry of *separation* at the laver, the ministry *of illumination* at the golden candlestick, the ministry of *satisfaction* at the table of showbread, the ministry of *intercession* at the altar of incense, and the ministry of *communion* at the ark of the covenant in the holy of holies.

As perfect High Priest, He also offers gifts and sacrifices. The sacrificial system of the Old Testament has perplexed many by its apparent complexity and wealth of detail, but we must not be put off by this. Underlying all these minute instructions and descriptions there is a wonderful prefiguring of the redeeming work of our great High Priest, the Lord Jesus Christ. In Hebrews 5:1 we are told that the high priest "is ordained . . . that he may offer both gifts and sacrifices for sins." The gifts represented the dedicatory offerings, while the sacrifices represented the substitutionary offerings. A gift might be a bloodless offering, as in the case of the meal offering. A sacrifice on account of sin necessitated blood shedding, because "without shedding of blood is no remission" (Hebrews 9:22).

In the first five chapters of the book of Leviticus, we have instructions and descriptions concerning the five different offerings that were to be presented to God. Three of these offerings were of the nature of gifts. They were called the burnt offering, the meal offering, and the peace offering. The last two were of the nature of sacrifices: namely, the sin offering and the trespass offering. Later on we shall be particularizing on the offerings, so we need not say more here by way of explanation and application.

In summing up, all that need be noted is that whether gifts or sacrifices, these offerings all speak supremely of Christ. Christ's death was both dedicatory and substitutionary. As Offerer and Offering, He gave Himself, first and foremost, as a *gift* of dedication to His Father. So Paul tells us that "Christ . . . hath given Himself for us an offering and a sacrifice to God for a sweetsmelling savour" (Ephesians 5:2). Then as Offerer and Offering, He gave Himself as a *sacrifice* on account of sins. Thus we read: "Who His own self bare our sins in His own body on the tree, that we, being dead to sins, should live unto righteousness" (1 Peter 2:24).

In this mysterious substitutionary offering no one could share. It was a work peculiar to Himself. But in the dedicatory offering we all can share, hence the entreaty of the

Apostle Paul when he says: "I beseech you ... by the mercies of God, that ye present your bodies a living sacrifice, holy, acceptable unto God, which is your reasonable service" (Romans 12:1).

So we have seen that the purpose of the Tabernacle, in its immediate aspect, was that of providing a place of worship and witness for the children of Israel in the wilderness, while the ultimate intention was that of prefiguring Christ in all the glory of His Person and the greatness of His work. May God give us anointed eyes to see beauty in His Person and blessedness in the work which He has accomplished once and for all for those who believe, and so may He become increasingly precious to us (1 Peter 2:7).

# Chapter 3

## THE ERECTION

*Scriptures for Study*

And the LORD spake unto Moses, saying, Speak unto the children of Israel, that they bring Me an offering: of every man that giveth it willingly with his heart ye shall take My offering. And this is the offering which ye shall take of them; gold, and silver, and brass, and blue, and purple, and scarlet, and fine linen, and goats' hair, and rams' skins dyed red, and badgers' skins, and shittim wood, Oil for the light, spices for anointing oil, and for sweet incense, Onyx stones, and stones to be set in the ephod, and in the breastplate. And let them make Me a sanctuary; that I may dwell among them. According to all that I show thee, after the pattern of the tabernacle, and the pattern of all the instruments thereof, even so shall ye make it (Exodus 25:1-9).

And the LORD spake unto Moses, saying, See, I have called by name Bezaleel the son of Uri, the son of Hur, of the tribe of Judah: and I have filled him with the spirit of God, in wisdom, and in understanding, and in knowledge, and in all manner of workmanship, To devise cunning works, to work in gold, and in silver, and in brass, and in cutting of stones, to set them, and in carving of timber, to work in all manner of workmanship. And I, behold, I have given with him Aholiab, the son of Ahisamach, of the tribe of Dan: and in the hearts of all that are wise hearted I have put wisdom, that they may make all that I have commanded thee; The tabernacle of the congregation, and the ark of the testimony, and the mercy seat that is thereupon, and all the furniture of the tabernacle, and the table and his furniture, and the pure candlestick with all his furniture, and the altar of incense, and the altar of burnt offering with all his furniture, and the laver and his foot, and the cloths of service, and the holy garments for Aaron the priest, and the garments of his sons, to minister in the priest's office, and the anointing oil, and sweet incense for the holy place: according to all that I have commanded thee shall they do (Exodus 31:1-11).

And all the congregation of the children of Israel departed from the presence of Moses. And they came, every one whose heart stirred him up, and every one whom his spirit made willing, and they brought the LORD'S offering to the work of the tabernacle of the congregation, and for all his service, and for the holy garments. And they came, both men and women, as many as were willing hearted, and brought brace-lets, and earrings, and rings, and tablets, all jewels of gold: and every man that offered offered an offering of gold unto the LORD. And every man, with whom was found blue, and purple, and scarlet, and fine linen, and goats' hair, and red skins of rams, and badgers' skins, brought them. Every one that did offer an offering of silver and brass brought the LORD'S offering: and every man, with whom was found shittim wood for any work of the service, brought it. And all the women that were wise hearted did spin with their hands, and brought that which they had spun, both of blue, and of purple, and of scarlet, and of fine linen. And all the women whose heart stirred them up in wisdom spun goats' hair. And the rulers brought onyx stones, and stones to be set, for the ephod, and for the breastplate; And spice, and oil for the light, and for the anointing oil, and for the sweet incense. The children of Israel brought a willing offering unto the LORD, every man and woman, whose heart made them willing to bring for all manner of work, which the LORD had commanded to be made by the hand of Moses (Exodus 35:20-29).

And they spake unto Moses, saying, The people bring much more than enough for the service of the work, which the LORD commanded to make. And Moses gave commandment, and they caused it to be proclaimed throughout the camp, saying, Let neither man nor woman make any more work for the offering of the sanctuary. So the people were restrained from bringing. For the stuff they had was sufficient for all the work to make it, and too much (Exodus 36:5-7).

And it came to pass in the first month in the second year, on the
first day of the month, that the tabernacle was reared up. . . . And he
reared up the court round about the tabernacle and the altar, and set up
the hanging of the court gate. So Moses finished the work.

Then a cloud covered the tent of the congregation, and the glory of
the LORD filled the tabernacle. And Moses was not able to enter into
the tent of the congregation, because the cloud abode thereon, and the
glory of the LORD filled the tabernacle. And when the cloud was taken
up from over the tabernacle, the children of Israel went onward in all
their journeys: But if the cloud were not taken up, then they journeyed
not till the day that it was taken up. For the cloud of the LORD was
upon the tabernacle by day, and the fire was on it by night, in the sight
of all the house of Israel, throughout all their journeys (Exodus
40:17,33-38).

### THE ERECTION

Scriptures for Study: Exodus 25:1-9; 31:1-11; 35:20-29; 36:5-7;
40:17,33-38

### I. GOD'S PATTERN FOR ITS ERECTION

1. Heavenly

2. Orderly

### II. GOD'S PROVISION FOR ITS ERECTION

1. The Materials
    a. The Donation of the Materials
    b. The Diversity of the Materials

2. The Man Power

### III.  GOD'S POSITION FOR ITS ERECTION

1.  In Relation to the Compass

2.  In Relation to the Camp

### IV.  GOD'S PERIOD FOR ITS ERECTION

1.  Its Commencement

2.  Its Completion


The story of the erection of the Tabernacle is one not only of spiritual significance but also of scientific magnificence. It is the record of a building which was perfect in every detail. Once completed, it never again required attention, addition, or alteration. So carefully and durably was it constructed that it lasted nearly five hundred years, including forty in the waste and howling wilderness. The only explanation for an erection of this quality is that God was behind its conception, as well as its construction.

Observe how this can be amplified and illustrated by four important considerations:


### I.  GOD'S PATTERN FOR ITS ERECTION

Both Old and New Testaments make it abundantly evident that the pattern for the erection of the Tabernacle was heavenly, and therefore orderly.

1.  Heavenly

God's instruction to Moses was: "Let them make Me a sanctuary; that I may dwell among them. According to all that I show thee, after the pattern of the tabernacle, and the pattern of all the instruments thereof, even so shall ye make it" (Exodus 25:8-9).

In one form or another that divine commandment was repeated again and again; for example: "Look that thou make them after their pattern, which was showed thee in the mount" (Exodus 25:40). And again: "Thou shalt rear up the tabernacle according to the fashion thereof which was showed thee in the mount" (Exodus 26:30, see also 27:8; Numbers 8:4; Acts 7:44; Hebrews 8:5).

The Tabernacle appears to have been an exact replica of something which already existed in Heaven. It is certainly plainly stated that Moses saw it (Hebrews 8:5). And it is not without significance that the same pattern was later shown to John while he was on the isle called Patmos, for we discover in the book of the Revelation an altar of sacrifice (6:9), a "sea of glass" (4:6), "seven golden candlesticks" (1:12), a "golden altar" (8:3), "hidden manna" (2:17), and "the ark of His testament" (11:19). Whether such a building does exist in Heaven is a debatable point. Of one thing, however, we are quite sure: the conception and construction of the Tabernacle was not the product of man, but of God Himself. The whole thing was a revelation. Rationalism could add nothing to what was revealed on the holy mount.

So we find three chapters containing full and precise instructions for the erection of the Tabernacle: that is, Exodus 25, 26, and 27. Then three chapters showing how fully and faithfully these instructions were carried out to the very letter: that is, Exodus 36, 37, and 38. The first three are chapters of command; the second three chapters of obedience. This is always God's way with man. What He reveals from Heaven constitutes His commands and demands unqualified obedience. The whole scheme of redemption has been shown us on the mount of Calvary. There, and there alone, have we the pattern for living. So Peter tells us: "Hereunto were ye called: because Christ also suffered for us, leaving us an example, that [we] should follow His steps" (1 Peter 2:21).

2. Orderly

Because the pattern is heavenly, it must of necessity be orderly. Such orderliness is evidenced in the physical structure, as well as the spiritual significance, of the Tabernacle. As we shall see in a future chapter, every single piece of this amazing structure had its own place. Like a jigsaw puzzle, each part exactly fitted its counterpart until the whole erection was complete. Detailed instructions were given as to the erecting, dismantling, and transporting of the Tabernacle. Then, of course, there is an orderliness in the spiritual significance. It is important to note that God began where man would end. We would complete the Tabernacle before giving attention to the furniture, whereas God commences with the most important piece of furniture, namely, the ark of the covenant. The divine movement is from within to without. Notice, once again, those words that have become almost our key text: "And let them make Me a sanctuary; that I may dwell among them. According to all that I show thee, after the pattern of the tabernacle. . . . *And they shall make an ark*" (Exodus 25:1-10). Why did the ark come first? Simply because the ark essentially represented the Person and presence of God; and God must be first. Personal, social, national, and international life goes wrong when that order is reversed. God must ever and always come first.

So we learn from the pattern of the Tabernacle that ours is the God of order. The word to us is: "Let all things be done decently and in order" (1 Corinthians 14:40).

## II. GOD'S PROVISION FOR ITS ERECTION

In general terms, this provision amounted to materials and man power.

1. The Materials

In His wise forethought, God saw to it that the children of Israel came out of Egypt with such materials as would later be required for the construction and erection of the Tabernacle. His instruction to the people, on the eve of their departure for the promised land, was: "Let every man borrow of his neighbour, and every woman of her neighbour, jewels of silver, and jewels of gold" (Exodus 11:2). We read that "the children of Israel did according to the word of Moses; and they borrowed of the Egyptians jewels of silver, and jewels of gold, and raiment: And the LORD gave the people favour in the sight of the Egyptians, so that they lent unto them such things as they required. And they spoiled the Egyptians" (12:35-36). The word "borrow" literally means "ask" or "request," so that in no way were the Israelites obligated to repay the Egyptians. Indeed, they had served them as slaves for hundreds of years, so that they were merely asking for their deferred pay and obtaining it.

So Moses took away with him from the land of the Pharaohs not only his learning and intellectual attainments, but also two-and-a-half million people, laden with valuables and jewelry to be used in the service of God as and when occasion arose. About four-and-a-half months later the call of God to give was proclaimed throughout the camp. What immediately transpired is a story almost too wonderful for words:

a. *The Donation of the Materials.* We read that "they came, every one whose heart stirred him up, and every one whom his spirit made willing, and they brought the LORD'S offering to the work of the tabernacle of the congregation, and for all his service, and for the holy garments" (Exodus 35:21). Such was the abundance of giving that the next chapter records: "Moses gave commandment, and they caused it to be proclaimed throughout the camp, saying, Let neither man nor woman make any more work for the offering of the sanctuary. So the people were restrained from bringing. For the stuff they had was sufficient for all the work to make it, and too much" (36:6-7).

We have here the evidence of true spirituality and liberality. It is of first importance to remember that everything offered to God must proceed from a heart made willing by His Spirit. It must be spontaneous and not merely a result of external persuasion. The Church of Christ would be in a very different state today if her giving were characterized by spirituality.

It is so instructive to note that in Paul's references to the grace of giving, he is careful to emphasize the indissoluble link between the Spirit-stirred heart and the liberal hand: "Every man according as he purposeth in his heart, so let him give; not grudgingly, or of necessity: for God loveth a cheerful giver" (2 Corinthians 9:7). Nothing could be further from the truth than to suggest that the ministry of giving was purely a mundane matter, unrelated to the things of the Spirit. When giving is characterized by spirituality, we can expect liberality.

We have already seen that such was the generosity of these willing-hearted people that their giving had to be restrained. It has been estimated that their voluntary contributions, not counting labor, amounted to nearly a million dollars in our money. The true test of spirituality is liberality of this quality, as well as quantity. The spiritually-minded man or woman has to say with David of old: "But who am I, and what is my people, that we should be able to offer so willingly after this sort? for all things come of Thee, and of Thine own have we given Thee" (1 Chronicles 29:14).

Such a spirit as this has always characterized God's people in times of revival. Think particularly of the early days of the Church, where we read that "all that believed were together, and had all things common; And sold their possessions and goods, and parted them to all men, as every man had need" (Acts 2:44-45). "Neither was there any among them that lacked: for as many as were possessors of lands or houses sold them, and brought the prices of the things that were sold, and laid them down at the apostles' feet" (Acts 4:34-35). The only recorded exception to this liberality was visited with divine judgment, as we see illustrated in the persons of Ananias and Sapphira, who agreed to hold back part of the price (see Acts 5:1-11).

With the donation of the materials, consider briefly:

b. *The Diversity of the Materials.* In *metals,* there was gold and silver and copper; in *colors,* blue, purple, and scarlet; in *fabrics,* fine linen, goats' hair, rams' skins, and badgers' skins; in *wood,* precious incorruptible acacia; in oil, both anointing and lighting oils; in *spices,* a rich variety for use in the anointing oil and for sweet incense; in *stones,* precious and rare stones for use in the high priest's ephod and breastplate. It was the sort of giving that left no one out. The rich gave gold and silver; the poor contributed goats' hair. For those who had no substance there was the giving of skill and labor. What an example this should be to us today!

> What shall I bring to the Saviour?
> What shall I lay at His feet?
> I have no glittering jewels,
> Gold, or frankincense so sweet.
>
> Gifts to the Saviour I'm bringing,
> Love's richest treasure to lay
> Low at His feet with rejoicing,
> Ere yonder sunset today.

What shall I bring to the Saviour?
Lips His dear praises to sing,
Feet that will walk in the pathway
Leading to Jesus, our King.

What shall I bring to the Saviour?
Love that is purest and best;
Life in its sweetness and beauty,
All for His service so blest.

## 2. The Man Power

"The LORD spake unto Moses, saying, See, I have called by name Bezaleel the son of Uri, the son of Hur, of the tribe of Judah: And I have filled him with the spirit of God, in wisdom, and in understanding, and in knowledge, and in all manner of workmanship. . . . And I, behold, I have given with him Aholiab, the son of Ahisamach, of the tribe of Dan: and in the hearts of all that are wise hearted I have put wisdom, that they may make all that I have commanded thee" (Exodus 31:1-3,6).

Here was workmanship by divine appointment and with divine equipment. Far from being illiterate, as some modernists have suggested, these men could build and practice arts in a manner which equals anything that we can do today.

Bezaleel, whose name means "in the shadow of God," beautifully illustrates the ministry of the Holy Spirit as the great Overseer in this present day of grace. Like the Holy Spirit, Bezaleel gave "to every man his work." He alone had the right "to devise curious works, to work in gold, and in silver, and in brass," (Exodus 35:32). Under his superintendence operated every wise-hearted man and woman (see Exodus 35:10,25) until the Tabernacle was completed to the glory of Jehovah.

God's method of operation is still the same today. Paul tells us that there are "diversities of gifts, but the same Spirit.

And there are differences of administrations, but the same Lord. And there are diversities of operations, but it is the same God which worketh all in all. But the manifestation of the Spirit is given to every man to profit withal" (1 Corinthians 12:4-7). In simple terms:

> There's a work for Jesus,
>   Ready at your hand;
> 'Tis the task the Master
>   Just for you has planned.
> Haste to do His bidding,
>   Yield Him service true;
> There's a work for Jesus
>   None but *you* can do.

Elsie Duncan Yale

God make us each faithful to our appointed tasks!


## III. GOD'S POSITION FOR ITS ERECTION

In his book on the Tabernacle, C. W. Slemming tells us that the Bedouins of the desert in Moses' day, as today, moved from place to place under their sheik, or chieftain. The chieftain leads the way on his camel, or Arab steed, carrying his fifteen- to twenty-foot-long spear in hand. When he wants to settle, he just plants his spear into the ground. That is the sign of rest. His servants then immediately erect their master's tent behind the spear; and pitch their own tents around in a circle or circles, according to the size of the camp. The sheik thus dwells in the midst of his people. When he desires to move on, he removes his spear and rides forth.

What a beautiful picture this is of the God of the children of Israel! As Chieftain, He led His people throughout those years of wandering. His spear was the pillar of cloud and of fire. When it moved, they moved. Thus the position of the Tabernacle was determined by the planting of that divine spear.

Notice its position:

1. In Relation to the Compass

The Tabernacle in the wilderness always faced east. It looked towards the sunrising. This should ever be the attitude of the believer and of the Church. Our outlook should be eastward, towards the sunrising, from whence the Lord will make His appearance. Jesus said: "As the lightning cometh out of the east, and shineth even unto the west; so shall also the coming of the Son of man be" (Matthew 24:27).

2. In Relation to the Camp

The Tabernacle was always to be central, with an encampment of some two-and-a-half million people covering a circuit of some twelve miles (see Numbers 2; 3:13-48). In carefully prescribed formation, the tents were pitched as follows:

On the *east* were the tents of Issachar 54,400; Judah 74,600; Zebulun 57,400 men (Numbers 2:3-9); on the *west* were the tents of Manasseh 32,200; Ephraim 40,500; Benjamin 35,400 men (Numbers 2:18-24); on the *north* were the tents of Asher 41,500; Dan 62,700; Naphtali 53,400 men (Numbers 2:25-31); on the *south* were the tents of Simeon 59,300; Reuben 46,500; Gad 45,650 men (Numbers 2:10-16).

Then flanking the Tabernacle on all sides was the tribe of Levi, divided into four families: on the *east,* Moses, Aaron, and the sons of Aaron the priests; on the *west,* the Gershonites 7,500; on the *north,* the Merarites 6,200; on the *south,* the Kohathites 8,600 (Numbers 1:47-54; 3:17-51).

Between the Tabernacle and the first line of tents there was a reserved space where the nation assembled before God for worship and instruction (see Numbers 2:2). People could not just push in and seize a place of vantage: they were obliged to accept direction (Numbers 1:52).

As we have seen, only one tribe was allowed to pitch its tents near to the Tabernacle: it was the tribe of Levi. To it was given the care and ministry of the Tabernacle. By this arrangement the Levites had a double responsibility: first, to keep the people from intrusion and thus preserve them, "that there be no wrath upon the congregation"; and secondly, to "keep the charge of the tabernacle of [the] testimony" (Numbers 1:53).

This orderly position of the camp was equaled only by the orderly formation when the children of Israel were on the march. The whole Tabernacle in its several pieces was carried in a specified order by specified persons. So impressive was the positioning and moving of these ancient pilgrims that their enemies were sore afraid when they looked upon them (see Numbers 22:3). Indeed, Balaam was so moved when he saw the beautiful order of the camp, as well as the glory of God, that instead of cursing the children of Israel he had to bless them (see Numbers 23:24).

The lesson we learn from the position of the Tabernacle in relation to the camp is that our Lord Jesus Christ, of whom the Tabernacle speaks, should be ever and always central in the life of the Christian and the Church. Paul reminds us that "He is the head of the body, the church . . . that in all things He might have the pre-eminence" (Colossians 1:18).

## IV. GOD'S PERIOD FOR ITS ERECTION

We have observed already in these studies that the erection of the Tabernacle had to follow God's act of redemption by blood and by power. Only after bringing the children of Israel out of Egypt into the wilderness could God say, "Speak unto the children of Israel. . . . And let them make Me a sanctuary; that I may dwell among them" (Exodus 25:2,8).

It is of further interest, however, to discover just when the making of the materials commenced, and at what point in time the completed Tabernacle was erected.

1. Its Commencement

It seems quite clear from reading the book of Exodus that it took two-and-a-half to three months to reach Mount Sinai: "In the third month, when the children of Israel were gone forth out of the land of Egypt, the same day came they into the wilderness of Sinai" (Exodus 19:1). They remained at the foot of Sinai forty days, for we read that "Moses was in the mount forty days and forty nights" (Exodus 24:18). That brings the time lapse to some four-and-a-half months.

It appears evident that it was after Moses came down from the mount that the work of making the Tabernacle began (see Exodus 34:32; 35:4,20,30). The date of its completion and erection was New Year's Day. "On the first day of the first month shalt thou set up the tabernacle of the tent of the congregation" (Exodus 40:2). And later we read: "In the first month in the second year, on the first day of the month . . . the tabernacle was reared up" (Exodus 40:17). Thus if we subtract four-and-a-half months from twelve, we have seven-and-a-half, suggesting that the actual making of the Tabernacle took something like seven-and-a-half to eight months.

2. Its Completion

As we have just seen, the Tabernacle was completed and erected on the first day of the first month, in the second year of the journeyings of the children of Israel: that is, over 3,000 years ago. It was set up on the anniversary of their departure from Egypt (Exodus 12:2). As their deliverance from the house of bondage constituted the commencement of their spiritual history, so the dwelling of Jehovah in their midst formed morally a new period of time.

These two facts are brought together in Christianity. When a soul is delivered from the bondage of sin to enjoy the pardon and peace of God, it is then that the Holy Spirit seals by the gift of His indwelling. With the commencement of spiritual life, the body also becomes the temple of the Holy Spirit. So we read: "Moses finished the work. Then a cloud covered the tent of the congregation, and the glory of the LORD filled the tabernacle. And Moses was not able to enter into the tent of the congregation, because the cloud abode thereon, and the glory of the LORD filled the tabernacle" (Exodus 40:33-35).

This happened at the completion of the Temple (see 2 Chronicles 5:13-14). Both the completion of the Tabernacle and the Temple are typical of what happened on Pentecost, for "when the day of Pentecost was fully come, they were all with one accord in one place. And suddenly there came a sound from heaven as of a rushing mighty wind, and it filled all the house where they were sitting" (Acts 2:1-4).

God always blesses with His Spirit and glory that which represents the completion of obedience. The Tabernacle represented the obedience of God's people to divine commands; so did the Temple. On the day of Pentecost the disciples were gathered together in obedience to the Lord's commands, so the Spirit fell upon them. How true are Peter's words, when later he says: "The Holy Ghost, whom God hath given to them that obey Him" (Acts 5:32).

So we have seen the rich lessons that emerge from a consideration of the erection of the Tabernacle. What was true physically of the Tabernacle can be true spiritually of your life and mine. God has a pattern, a provision, a position, and a period for His purpose of blessing for each of us. Let us see to it that we do not miss the blessing or the glory.

# Chapter 4

## THE STRUCTURE

### *Scriptures for Study*

Moreover thou shalt make the tabernacle with ten curtains of fine twined linen, and blue, and purple, and scarlet: with cherubims of cunning work shalt thou make them. . . . And thou shalt make boards for the tabernacle of shittim wood standing up. . . . And thou shalt make bars of shittim wood; five for the boards of the one side of the tabernacle. . . . And thou shalt overlay the boards with gold, and make their rings of gold for places for the bars: and thou shalt overlay the bars with gold. . . . And thou shalt make a vail of blue, and purple, and scarlet, and fine twined linen of cunning work: with cherubims shall it be made: And thou shalt hang it upon four pillars of shittim wood overlaid with gold: their hooks shall be of gold, upon the four sockets of silver (Exodus 26:1-32).

And thou shalt make the court of the tabernacle: for the south side southward there shall be hangings for the court of fine twined linen of an hundred cubits long for one side: And the twenty pillars thereof and their twenty sockets shall be of brass; the hooks of the pillars and their fillets shall be of silver. And likewise for the north side in length there shall be hangings of an hundred cubits long, and his twenty pillars and their twenty sockets of brass; the hooks of the pillars and their fillets of silver. And for the breadth of the court on the west side shall be hangings of fifty cubits: their pillars ten, and their sockets ten. And the breadth of the court on the east side eastward shall be fifty cubits. The hangings of one side of the gate shall be fifteen cubits: their pillars three, and their sockets three. And on the other side shall be hangings fifteen cubits: their pillars three, and their sockets three. And for the gate of the court shall be an hanging of twenty cubits, of blue, and purple, and scarlet, and fine twined linen, wrought with needlework: and their pillars shall be four, and their sockets four. All the pillars round about the court shall be filleted with silver; their hooks shall be of silver, and their sockets of brass. The length of the court shall be an hundred cubits, and the breadth fifty every where, and the height five cubits of fine twined linen, and their sockets of brass (Exodus 27:9-18).

And every wise hearted man among them that wrought the work of the tabernacle made ten curtains of fine twined linen, and blue, and purple, and scarlet: with cherubims of cunning work made he them. . . . And he made curtains of goats' hair for the tent over the tabernacle: eleven curtains he made them. . . . And he made boards for the tabernacle of shittim wood, standing up. . . . And he made bars of shittim wood; five for the boards of the one side of the tabernacle, and five bars for the boards of the other side of the tabernacle, and five bars for the boards of the tabernacle for the sides westward. . . . And he made a vail of blue, and purple, and scarlet, and fine twined linen: with cherubims made he it of cunning work. . . . And he made an hanging for the tabernacle door of blue, and purple, and scarlet, and fine twined linen, of needlework; And the five pillars of it with their hooks: and he overlaid their chapiters and their fillets with gold: but their five sockets were of brass (Exodus 36:8-38; see also Exodus 38:9-20).

## THE STRUCTURE

Scriptures for Study: Exodus 26:1-32; 27:9-18; 36:8-38; 38:9-20

### I. THE CURTAINED ENCLOSURE

1. The Scriptural Specifications
   a. The Dimensions of the Enclosure
   b. The Description of the Enclosure

## II. THE CENTRAL ERECTION

## III. THE COVERED ENTRANCES

Our study of the structure of the Tabernacle will be concerned with the curtained enclosure, known as the court or courtyard; the central erection, or the Tabernacle itself; and the covered entrances, which are referred to as the gate, the door, and the veil. In each of these considerations we shall look first at the scriptural specifications and then at the spiritual significance, as it relates to our Lord Jesus Christ and to ourselves. May our eyes and our hearts be anointed to see and obey such truths as will emerge.

## I. THE CURTAINED ENCLOSURE

### (Exodus 27:9-18; 38:9-20)

First of all, let us note:

1. The Scriptural Specifications

"And thou shalt make the court of the tabernacle" (Exodus 27:9). In these scriptural specifications we have:

a. *The Dimensions of the Enclosure.* The court was to be one hundred cubits long, fifty cubits wide, and five cubits high. There has been much diversity of opinion as to the English measurement of the cubit, but it is generally accepted that it is twenty-and-one-half inches. With this in mind, those interested can work out their own measurements. The important thing is to observe that it was twice as long as its breadth, and too high for any normal man to look over.

The structure of the court contained sixty pillars; sixty chapiters, or silver caps, for the pillars; sixty brass sockets; a hundred and twenty cords and brass pins; sixty silver fillets or connecting bars; and one thousand four hundred square cubits of fine twined linen (excluding the curtains of the gate).

b. *The Description of the Enclosure.* The courtyard of the Tabernacle was an uncovered area of dimensions already given. It was surrounded by a curtain of fine twined linen, attached by silver hooks to sixty pillars. These pillars, presumably of acacia wood (although this is not specifically stated) were silver capped and fixed into sixty sockets of brass, which were buried in the sand. The pillars were kept at an equal distance apart by silver connecting bars, and held erect by cords and brass tent pegs.

Now let us look at:

2. The Spiritual Significance

There are seven matters of importance, referred to in the specifications, which deserve our attention. Each has a spiritual significance which we do well to consider seriously:

a. *The Linen.* As we have seen, the hangings in the court were one thousand four hundred square cubits of fine twined linen, excluding the embroidered curtains of the gate. From the outside this expanse of white linen must have looked most impressive. It speaks of *righteousness,* for Revelation 19:8 tells us that "fine linen is the righteousness of saints." This righteousness of saints is imputed and imparted by God, through our Lord Jesus Christ. "Christ Jesus . . . is made unto us wisdom, and righteousness, and sanctification, and redemption" (1 Corinthians 1:30). Human righteousness is nothing less than "filthy rags," the Prophet Isaiah tells us (64:6). So we see in that curtained enclosure a picture of the life of our Lord Jesus, who was "holy, harmless, undefiled, separate from sinners" (Hebrews 7:26).

In a secondary way, we also see the believer in his witness to the outside world; for every one of us should be "found in Him, not having [our] own righteousness, which is of the law, but that which is through the faith of Christ, the righteousness which is of God by faith" (Philippians 3:9). Our duty before God and men is to deny "ungodliness and worldly lusts" and to "live soberly, righteously, and godly, in this present world" (Titus 2:12). For this very purpose we have been redeemed.

b. *The Pillars.* These, so far as we can judge, were of imperishable acacia wood, and speak of the perfect *humanity* of our Lord. When the angel announced the birth of the Lord

Jesus, he said: "That holy thing which shall be born of thee shall be called the Son of God" (Luke 1:35). No wonder it was not possible for His body to see corruption (Acts 2:31)!

To a lesser extent, these pillars also speak of the believer, whose life has been cut off from the world outside, shaped and fashioned to become a pillar in the house of God. Paul describes the Church of the living God as "the pillar and ground of the truth" (1 Timothy 3:15).

c. *The Sockets.* These were of brass, and speak of perfect *endurance* in the fires of judgment. In the vision given us of the Lord Jesus in the book of the Revelation, we read that "His feet [were] like unto fine brass, as if they burned in a furnace" (1:15). So the basis of the gospel testimony in the world is the enduring obedience of the Lord Jesus that went through death and emerged in resurrection. We read that Jesus "endured the cross, despising the shame, and is set down at the right hand of the throne of God" (Hebrews 12:2).

As pillars in the Church, we, too, must be "fixed" or characterized by steadfast endurance, if our witness is to tell in the world. So we are told to "stand fast in the Lord" (Philippians 4:1); and again, to be "stedfast, unmoveable, always abounding in the work of the Lord" (1 Corinthians 15:58).

d. *The Chapiters.* These were the silver caps which were attached to the top of each pillar. All silver used in the building of the Tabernacle was melted down from redemption money. This was the half-shekel that every man over twenty had to pay for the ransom of his soul (see Exodus 30:12-16). Thus, silver speaks ever and always of *redemption;* and therefore of the Captain of our salvation.

If the brass sockets speak of endurance in judgment, then the silver caps denote the experience of salvation. In all our witness to the Saviour, we must see to it that we neglect not the "so great salvation" (Hebrews 2:3), which God has made available to us through wondrous grace.

The other silver items in the structure of the court were the *connecting bars* and the *hooks*. In the connecting bars, we see again the outworking of the Redeemer's purpose in keeping His people in fellowship with one another. So the Word reminds us: "If we walk in the light, as He is in the light, we have fellowship one with another, and the blood of Jesus Christ His Son cleanseth us from all sin" (1 John 1:7).

The *silver hooks* held up the curtains, and so teach us that only on the basis of His cross work can God's saving righteousness be displayed to a world of need. Paul speaks of Christ Jesus, "Whom God hath set forth to be a propitiation through faith in His blood, to declare His righteousness" (Romans 3:25). In a similar way, the link between ourselves and the righteousness we seek to preach is a crucified Saviour. So Paul could tell the Corinthians: "I determined not to know any thing among you, save Jesus Christ, and Him crucified" (1 Corinthians 2:2).

e. *The Pegs.* These were made of brass and driven into the ground. As we have seen already, this metal speaks of endurance through judgment; and so of the Lord Jesus as one who went down into death and rose again. The peg beneath the ground is a symbol of the death of Christ, while the part above the ground suggests His resurrection. How wonderful to know that "if we have been planted together in the likeness of His death, we shall be also in the likeness of His resurrection" (Romans 6:5). By the power of Christ's death and resurrection we can know an endurance capable of withstanding the elements of desert life.

In the Bible these tent pegs are called "nails" and in another place "stakes." In Isaiah 22:23-24 there is a direct reference to our Lord as a nail. We read: "I will fasten Him as a nail in a sure place; and He shall be for a glorious throne to

His father's house. And they shall hang upon Him all the glory of His father's house." Praise God, we share in this security and glory!

f. *The Cords.* The tent pegs and cords were used for the securing of the pillars of the outer enclosure. Without doubt, these cords speak of the infinite *love* of the Lord Jesus. Speaking of His people in Hosea's day, Jehovah says: "I drew them with cords of a man, with bands of love" (Hosea 11:4). Because we can say "the Son of God, who loved me, and gave Himself for me" (Galatians 2:20) we cannot but love Him back. John reminds us: "We love Him, because He first loved us" (1 John 4:19). It is only such constraining love that keeps us erect in our witness and anchored to a life of endurance.

So we have seen something of the more detailed significance of the different aspects of the structure of the court. In general terms, the purpose of this enclosure was to keep man out. Man's approach to the Tabernacle where God dwelt could only be by means of the "one Door, and only one." To come through that gate meant confronting the place of sacrifice and forgiveness of sin. While the curtained enclosure excluded the sinner, it protected the believer for purposes of worship and witness.

Now we turn to the second structure, namely:

## II.  THE CENTRAL ERECTION

### (Exodus 26; 36:8-38)

To start with, let us look at:

1.  The Scriptural Specifications

"Moreover thou shalt make the tabernacle" (Exodus 26:1). In these scriptural specifications we have:

a. *The Dimensions of the Erection.* It was thirty cubits long, ten cubits wide, and ten cubits high. The material used included a hundred silver sockets, forty-eight boards size ten by one-and-a-half cubits, fifteen bars, ten curtains, fifty taches or clips, a hundred blue loops.

b. *The Description of the Erection.* The Tabernacle stood on the west side of the court, in line with the gate. The solid framework was composed of forty-eight boards — twenty on the north, twenty on the south, and eight on the west side (including the two corner boards). These boards were of acacia wood, overlaid with gold, having two tenons or feet which were inserted into ninety-six silver sockets, two sockets for each board. Each of these sockets weighed approximately a hundred and twenty-five pounds, thus the estimated total of the silver sockets was something like five-and-a-half tons. The boards were held together by fifteen bars on each of the three sides of the Tabernacle. These wooden bars, overlaid with gold, passed through a series of rings which were in the boards.

On the east side of the Tabernacle was a door, made of fine twined linen, embroidered in blue, purple, and scarlet, and suspended on five pillars, each resting on a socket of brass. A veil of the same size, materials, and colors (except for beautifully wrought cherubim), hung on four pillars set into sockets of silver. This veil constituted a partition between the only two rooms in the Tabernacle: namely, the holy place (twenty cubits by ten cubits), and the holy of holies (a perfect cube of ten cubits).

Over the wooden structure was a roof of four coverings: the first, of fine twined linen; the second, of cloth made of goats' hair; the third, of rams' skins dyed red; and the fourth, of badgers' skins.

2. The Spiritual Significance

The significance of a good deal of the material used in the

Tabernacle itself has been already touched upon in our consideration of the courtyard. It only remains to point out something of the meaning of the base, boards, and bars of the Tabernacle:

a. *The Base.* As we have seen in the detailed dimensions, something like a hundred sockets of silver were used as a base for the structure of the Tabernacle. This was atonement money, as we noted earlier, and speaks of the redeeming work of Christ upon which our salvation rests.

Without doubt, Peter had in mind the Tabernacle when he wrote: "Forasmuch as ye know that ye were not redeemed with corruptible things, as silver and gold, from your vain conversation received by tradition from your fathers; But with the precious blood of Christ, as of a lamb without blemish and without spot" (1 Peter 1:18-19). With that redeeming work as our basis of faith, we can say: "If God be for us, who can be against us? . . . Who shall lay any thing to the charge of God's elect? It is God that justifieth. Who is he that condemneth? It is Christ that died, yea rather, that is risen again, who is even at the right hand of God, who also maketh intercession for us" (Romans 8:31,33-34).

b. *The Boards.* Moses was told: "Thou shalt make boards for the tabernacle of shittim wood standing up" (Exodus 26:15). These boards speak of Christ in His perfect humanity and deity: imperishable wood, covered with pure gold. How wonderfully He stands out before us in the Gospels as the Son of Man, as well as the Son of God.

These boards also speak to us of the believer who has been cut down, as was Saul of Tarsus on the way to Damascus, shaped and fashioned, and made a partaker of the divine nature (see 2 Peter 1:4).

Our right to be associated with the worship and witness of God is that we stand on redemption ground. Let us see to it, then, that our two feet are well fixed in the silver sockets.

So shall we cease to be as "children, tossed to and fro, and carried about with every wind of doctrine" (Ephesians 4:14).

    c. *The Bars.* The instructions to Moses were: "Thou shalt make bars of shittim wood. . . . And thou shalt overlay the boards with gold" (Exodus 26:26,29). There were fifteen of these bars, five for each of the sides: north, south, and west. The center bar went from one end to the other, while the others were apparently half lengths. Without doubt, these bars speak to us of the unifying work of the Holy Spirit. So we are exhorted to "keep the unity of the Spirit in the bond of peace" (Ephesians 4:3). As a result of this unifying ministry, the building of God is "fitly framed together [and] groweth unto an holy temple in the Lord: In whom," adds Paul, "ye also are builded together for an habitation of God through the Spirit" (Ephesians 2:21-22).

    There are those who see in the five bars a picture of five ministries of the Holy Spirit through men. In Ephesians 4:11 we read: "And He gave some, apostles; and some, prophets; and some, evangelists; and some, pastors and teachers." The first two represent the foundational ministry of the Church: namely, apostles and prophets (Ephesians 2:20). The middle bar represents the evangelist; it is the longest bar, going from end to end. His task is to go into all the world and preach the gospel to every creature (Mark 16:15). The two bars above answer to the task of the pastor and teacher. All these together are "For the perfecting of the saints, for the work of the ministry, for the edifying of the body of Christ: Till we all come in the unity of the faith, and of the knowledge of the Son of God, unto a perfect man, unto the measure of the stature of the fulness of Christ" (Ephesians 4:12-13).

    So we have seen how the Tabernacle bears the twofold testimony to Christ and the life of the believer.

    Now we turn to:

### III.  THE COVERED ENTRANCES

(Exodus 26:31-33,36-37; 27:16-17; 36:35-36; 38:9-19)

Once again, let us commence by observing:
1.  The Scriptural Specifications
     "And for the gate of the court shall be an hanging" (Exodus 27:16).
     "And thou shalt make an hanging for the door of the tent" (Exodus 26:36).
     "And thou shalt make a vail" (Exodus 26:31).
     In these scriptural specifications we have:
     a. *The Dimensions of the Entrances.* These were three in number:
> 1)  The Gate — twenty cubits wide, five cubits high
> 2)  The Door — ten cubits wide, ten cubits high (on five pillars)
> 3)  The Veil — ten cubits wide, ten cubits high

     b. *The Description of the Entrances.* The gate was the entrance into the outer court on the east side. The hangings of this gate were suspended on four pillars, probably of acacia wood, fixed in sockets of brass; the hooks, the connecting bars, and chapiters being of silver. This gate stood exactly in the center and was twenty cubits wide and only five cubits high, leaving ten cubits of enclosure on either side. The hanging was of fine twined linen, wrought in blue, purple, and scarlet.

     The door of the Tabernacle was of the same material and pattern, attached by gold hooks to five pillars, overlaid and capped with gold, and fixed in sockets of brass. The main differences to the gate were that there were five pillars instead of four, and that the height was ten cubits instead of five.

     The veil was another hanging of fine twined linen, with

the same pattern as the gate and the door, but with the added cherubim cunningly worked into the material. The veil was suspended by gold hooks on four pillars, overlaid with gold, fixed in the sockets of silver.

2. The Spiritual Significance

a. *The Gate.* The curtain which hung across this gate clearly speaks of the Lord Jesus in a fourfold aspect, for we are reminded that "the gate of the court shall be an hanging of twenty cubits, of blue, and purple, and scarlet, and fine twined linen, wrought with needlework: and their pillars shall be four, and their sockets four" (Exodus 27:16). This sets forth the Lord Jesus as:

> The divine Son — blue
> The divine Sovereign — purple
> The divine Saviour — scarlet
> The divine Servant — white

You will remember that Matthew speaks of Him as the divine Sovereign; Mark, as the divine Servant; Luke, as the divine Saviour; and John, as the divine Son. The four pillars might well represent the four apostles who set forth this fourfold picture of the Lord Jesus. The four also speaks of universality; and without doubt there is the thought here of the universal appeal of this wonderful Saviour. Matthew wrote for the Jews, Mark for the Romans, Luke for the Greeks, and John for the believers. So there is an attractiveness in the Lord Jesus for those who have eyes to see.

b. *The Door.* We read that Moses "made an hanging for the tabernacle door of blue, and purple, and scarlet, and fine twined linen, of needlework; And the five pillars of it with their hooks: and he overlaid their chapiters and their fillets with gold: but their five sockets were of brass" (Exodus 36:37-38). It seems fairly evident that the door here is a picture of the Lord Jesus as the door into a life of blessing. We must ever remember that when He said "I am the door:

by Me if any man enter in, he shall be saved, and shall go in and out, and find pasture" (John 10:9), He was speaking of His sheep. We may well use that text for the gospel, but its primary application is to His own people.

The material and pattern of the door was exactly the same as that of the gate. The only difference was that there were five pillars instead of four, and that these pillars were overlaid and crowned with gold. Five speaks of human responsibility and also of the grace of God. It is our responsibility as believers to enter fully into the enjoyment of God's sovereign grace. Paul speaks of this when he says: "Therefore being justified by faith, we have peace with God through our Lord Jesus Christ: By whom also we have access by faith into this grace wherein we stand, and rejoice in hope of the glory of God" (Romans 5:1-2).

The door of the Tabernacle was higher than the gate of five cubits, suggesting higher heights of the experience of God's saving and satisfying grace.

c. *The Veil.* Once again, God commanded His servant Moses, saying: "Thou shalt make a vail of blue, and purple, and scarlet, and fine twined linen of cunning work: with cherubims shall it be made: And thou shalt hang it upon four pillars of shittim wood overlaid with gold: their hooks shall be of gold, upon the four sockets of silver" (Exodus 26:31-32).

The veil was the curtain which shut off the holiest of all. Like the hangings of the gate and the door, it was of fine twined linen, with a similar pattern. The only difference was that Bezaleel, anointed by the Spirit, cunningly wrought cherubim on the linen. Tradition says that it was as thick as a hand's breadth.

We can be in no doubt as to the significance of the veil, for we read in the Epistle to the Hebrews that Jesus has consecrated for us a new and living way, through the veil, that is to say, His flesh (Hebrews 10:20). Just as Bezaleel, under the operation of the Holy Spirit, produced this wonderful curtain, so God, by the operation of the Holy Spirit, brought about miraculously that prepared body, which was to incarnate the Godhead. We read that the angel said to Mary: "The Holy Ghost shall come upon thee, and the power of the Highest shall overshadow thee: therefore also that holy thing which shall be born of thee shall be called the Son of God" (Luke 1:35).

Once again, the four pillars typify the apostles who tell the story of His earthly life, with special emphasis on His death. Some scholars see in the absence of chapters on these four pillars a hint of the life of Christ cut off.

The *Cherubim* are extremely difficult to interpret. Views have varied right down through the centuries. The obvious thing that can be said about them is that they were God's guardians. They appeared with flaming sword in the Garden of Eden, after the expulsion of Adam and Eve (Genesis 3:24). As we shall see later, they stood over the ark, to protect it; and here, worked in the veil, they represented God's sentinels against any unauthorized intrusion.

Only once a year did the high priest enter the holiest of all, and this in a strictly prescribed way. Thank God, however, that when Jesus cried, "It is finished!" on the cross, the veil of the Temple (materially different, but symbolically the same) was rent from top to bottom. The record tells us: "Behold, the veil of the temple was rent in twain from the top to the bottom" (Matthew 27:51). That means to say it was supernaturally rent — "rent in twain from the top." It was also completely rent — "rent in twain from the top to the bottom." Now, as believers, we can enter the holiest of all, none daring to make us afraid: for the Word says: "Having therefore, brethren, boldness to enter into the holiest by the blood of Jesus, By a new and living way, which

He hath consecrated for us, through the veil, that is to say, His flesh . . . Let us draw near with a true heart in full assurance of faith" (Hebrews 10:19-20,22).

We see, therefore, that each of these curtained entrances has a message for those who are prepared to follow the interpretations of the Holy Spirit. As we come to the conclusion of our study of the structure of the Tabernacle, we discover once again that in God's Temple "every whit of it uttereth His glory" (Psalm 29:9, margin). Gazing upon this glory, may we be changed into the image of the One of whom it speaks, "from glory to glory, even as by the Spirit of the Lord" (2 Corinthians 3:18).

# Chapter 5

## THE COVERINGS

### *Scriptures for Study*

Moreover thou shalt make the tabernacle with ten curtains of fine twined linen, and blue, and purple, and scarlet: with cherubims of cunning work shalt thou make them. The length of one curtain shall be eight and twenty cubits, and the breadth of one curtain four cubits: and every one of the curtains shall have one measure. The five curtains shall be coupled together one to another; and other five curtains shall be coupled one to another. And thou shalt make loops of blue upon the edge of the one curtain from the selvedge in the coupling; and likewise shalt thou make in the uttermost edge of another curtain, in the coupling of the second. Fifty loops shalt thou make in the one curtain, and fifty loops shalt thou make in the edge of the curtain that is in the coupling of the second; that the loops may take hold one of another. And thou shalt make fifty taches of gold, and couple the curtains together with the taches: and it shall be one tabernacle.

And thou shalt make curtains of goats' hair to be a covering upon the tabernacle: eleven curtains shalt thou make. The length of one curtain shall be thirty cubits, and the breadth of one curtain four cubits: and the eleven curtains shall be all of one measure. And thou shalt couple five curtains by themselves, and six curtains by themselves, and shalt double the sixth curtain in the forefront of the tabernacle. And thou shalt make fifty loops on the edge of the one curtain that is outmost in the coupling, and fifty loops in the edge of the curtain which coupleth the second. And thou shalt make fifty taches of brass, and put the taches into the loops, and couple the tent together, that it may be one. And the remnant that remaineth of the curtains of the tent, the half curtain that remaineth, shall hang over the backside of the tabernacle. And a cubit on the one side, and a cubit on the other side of that which remaineth in the length of the curtains of the tent, it shall hang over the sides of the tabernacle on this side and on that side, to cover it. And thou shalt make a covering for the tent of rams' skins dyed red, and a covering above of badgers' skins (Exodus 26:1-14).

And every wise hearted man among them that wrought the work of the tabernacle made ten curtains of fine twined linen, and blue, and purple, and scarlet: with cherubims of cunning work made he them. The length of one curtain was twenty and eight cubits, and the breadth of one curtain four cubits: the curtains were all of one size. And he coupled the five curtains one unto another: and the other five curtains he coupled one unto another. And he made loops of blue on the edge of one curtain from the selvedge in the coupling: likewise he made in the uttermost side of another curtain, in the coupling of the second. Fifty loops made he in one curtain, and fifty loops made he in the edge of the curtain which was in the coupling of the second: the loops held one curtain to another. And he made fifty taches of gold, and coupled the curtains one unto another with the taches: so it became one tabernacle.

And he made curtains of goats' hair for the tent over the tabernacle: eleven curtains he made them. The length of one curtain was thirty cubits, and four cubits was the breadth of one curtain: the eleven curtains were of one size. And he coupled five curtains by themselves, and six curtains by themselves. And he made fifty loops upon the uttermost edge of the curtain in the coupling, and fifty loops made he upon the edge of the curtain which coupleth the second. And he made fifty taches of brass to couple the tent together, that it might be one. And he made a covering for the tent of rams' skins dyed red, and a covering of badgers' skins above that (Exodus 36:8-19).

# THE COVERINGS

Scriptures for Study: Exodus 26:1-14; 36:8-19

## I. THE INNER CURTAINS

1. The Tabernacle
   a. The Scriptural Specifications
   b. The Spiritual Significance
      1) The Material
      2) The Measurements

2. The Tent
   a. The Scriptural Specifications
   b. The Spiritual Significance
      1) The Material
      2) The Measurements

## II. THE OUTER COVERINGS

1. The Rams' Skins
   a. The Scriptural Specifications
   b. The Spiritual Significance
      1) The Material
      2) The Measurements

2. The Seal Skins
   a. The Scriptural Specifications
      1) The Material
      2) The Measurements

The roof of the Tabernacle consisted of two inner curtains and two outer coverings, each being quite different from the other, and yet together making one composite whole. To study these coverings is to find that they all speak of the Lord Jesus, in terms of His glorious Person and victorious work. Like the four Gospels, each covering is complete in itself, but all are needed to give a full-toned testimony of the Saviour. As we examine the coverings, let us prayerfully count on the Holy Spirit to take of the things of Christ and show them unto us.

## I. THE INNER CURTAINS

### (Exodus 26:1-14; 36:8-19)

These were known, respectively, as "the tabernacle" (Exodus 26:6) and "the tent" (Exodus 26:11). As we study them, we shall note first the scriptural specifications and then the spiritual significance of each.

1. The Tabernacle

"Moreover thou shalt make the tabernacle with ten curtains of fine twined linen, and blue, and purple, and scarlet: with cherubims of cunning work shalt thou make them. . . . thou shalt make fifty taches of gold, and couple the curtains together with the taches: and it shall be one tabernacle" (Exodus 26:1,6).

This set of curtains was called "the tabernacle" because it actually comprised the roof of the main structure.

a. *The Scriptural Specifications.* The curtains were ten in number, each twenty-eight by four cubits. They were sewn together in two sets of five, and joined by a hundred blue loops and fifty golden taches, or clasps. The material was fine twined linen, worked in blue, purple, and scarlet, and further beautified by cunningly wrought cherubim. The complete curtain was stretched breadthwise across the Tabernacle, north to south. As the width of the sacred building was ten cubits, and the height ten cubits, this linen curtain left one cubit exposed on the north and south sides. Lengthwise, it covered the roof and the west side completely.

b. *The Spiritual Significance.* In our consideration of these coverings, we are commencing with the innermost curtain, which constituted the ceiling of the sacred building. It was seen only by those who ministered within the holy place, or holy of holies. In appearance it must have looked indescribably beautiful, and so fittingly represents the inner glory of the Lord Jesus Christ which is hidden from all but those who have eyes to see. In the days of His flesh there were occasions when His disciples pierced through the badgers' skins, rams' skins, and the curtain of goats' hair, and seeing His divine glory could say: "We beheld His glory, the glory as of the only begotten of the Father, full of grace and truth" (John 1:14). Peter, in particular, recalls his experience on the mount of Transfiguration where he witnessed the majesty of the Lord Jesus Christ (2 Peter 1:16). Before we proceed further, it is well to point out that we, too, may behold that glory, if we take advantage of our privilege as priests unto God and habituate not only the holy place, but the holy of holies.

To understand the spiritual significance of these curtains, we must study carefully the materials and the measurements.

1. *The Material.* We have noted in the specifications that the material of this inner curtain was fine twined linen, overpatterned with blue, purple, and scarlet, and embroidered with cherubim. Now these colors are already familiar to us, but it is fitting that we should remind ourselves of their spiritual meaning in relation to the Person and work of our Lord Jesus Christ.

The *linen* speaks of the purity of Christ's humanity. It was fine twined linen: that is to say, there was a variety in the unity of His personality. Every trait of perfect humanity was included in His make-up. Speaking of His birth, the angel could say: "That holy thing which shall be born of thee shall be called the Son of God" (Luke 1:35).

Looking back upon His life, the Apostle Paul could write: "Jesus Christ . . . was . . . declared to be the Son of God with power, according to the spirit of holiness, by the resurrection from the dead" (Romans 1:3-4).

Demons could declare: "We . . . know Thee who Thou art, the Holy One of God" (Mark 1:24).

The centurion at the cross confessed: "Certainly this was a righteous man" (Luke 23:47).

Well does John in his Epistle state that He is "Jesus Christ the righteous" (1 John 2:1).

The *blue* speaks of the mystery of Christ's divinity. We look up into the heavens and see the serene and unsullied blue of God. Clouds may come and clouds may go, but God's blue remains unaffected and untainted. And so as "The heavens declare the glory of God" (Psalm 19:1), the blue declares the divinity of Christ. How this divinity was embodied in flesh will ever be a mystery. "Great is the mystery of godliness: God was manifest in the flesh" (1 Timothy 3:16).

Jesus spoke of Himself as the living Bread sent down from Heaven (John 6:33). Speaking to Nicodemus, He said that He was "the Son of man which is in heaven" (John 3:13). And the apostle tells us that "the second man is the Lord from heaven" (1 Corinthians 15:47).

The *purple* speaks of the majesty of Christ's regality. Purple is the color of royalty, and declares the kingly character of our Lord Jesus Christ. Isaiah foretells the birth of this wonderful King when he says: "Unto us a child is born, unto us a son is given: and the government shall be upon His shoulder: and His name shall be called Wonderful, Counsellor, The mighty God, The everlasting Father, The Prince of

Peace. Of the increase of His government and peace there shall be no end, upon the throne of David, and upon His kingdom, to order it, and to establish it" (Isaiah 9:6-7).

In Psalm 2 we hear David putting words into the mouth of God, when he says in a context of world chaos and turmoil, "Yet have I set My king upon My holy hill of Zion" (verse 6).

During his lifetime, Matthew pierced through the outer coverings to discern the regal character of Jesus of Nazareth, and spoke of Him again and again as the King of the Jews; and so He was.

The Church today awaits His second coming, when it will be demonstrated universally that He is "the blessed and only Potentate, the King of kings, and Lord of lords" (1 Timothy 6:15).

This, then, is His purple character. God give us grace to know more of it in our personal lives.

The *scarlet* speaks of the quality of Christ's humility. There are three thoughts associated with this color of scarlet. In the first place, when God created our first parent, He gave him the name "Adam," which means "red earth." When the Lord Jesus would become our Saviour, we read that like the children of earth who are the "partakers of flesh and blood, He also Himself likewise took part of the same; that through death He might destroy him that had the power of death, that is, the devil; And deliver them who through fear of death were all their lifetime subject to bondage" (Hebrews 2:14-15).

Then those who know Palestine will realize that the earth of that country is red in color, and it was to this spot on God's earth that Jesus came. As the divine Servant and Saviour, He became humble enough to soil His feet with the dust of the Palestinian roads.

Once again, the word "scarlet" is rendered in the margin

of some Bibles as "worm scarlet," and, therefore, points to the brilliant color which is produced from the death of a certain insect (note Psalm 22:6). In other words, scarlet is a symbol of blood, and therefore of death. It singularly typifies the quality of the Saviour's humility, which caused Him to be "obedient unto death, even the death of the cross" (Philippians 2:8). What that humbling meant to the Saviour, none of the ransomed will ever know, but, thank God:

> He died that we might be forgiven,
> He died to make us good,
> That we might go at last to Heaven,
> Saved by His precious blood.
>
> Cecil F. Alexander

The *cherubim* speak of the intensity of Christ's severity. We have already observed in these studies that the cherubim are God's messengers of judgment and protection. They appeared with flaming sword in the Garden of Eden, after the expulsion of Adam and Eve (see Genesis 3:24). As cunningly embroidered on this inner curtain, they speak of the Lord Jesus in His severity of judgment. We must remember that, although He is the Lover of our souls and has died to redeem us to Himself, He is also the coming Judge of the world. The Scriptures make it plain that: "[God] hath appointed a day, in the which He will judge the world in righteousness by that man whom He hath ordained" (Acts 17:31). We also read that "the Father . . . hath committed all judgment unto the Son" (John 5:22). So we are exhorted to behold "the goodness and severity of God" (Romans 11:22).

Thus, in this glorious inner curtain, we have a full-length portrait of God's Son in His humanity, His divinity, His regality, His humility, and His severity in coming judgment. How incomparably glorious and victorious is the Christ of God!

You will notice that the two sets of curtains were made one whole by loops and clasps. The *blue loops,* once again, speak of His divine holiness, while the *gold clasps,* His divine righteousness. Holiness tells of what Jesus is in character, while righteousness represents His conduct. In the function of the loops and clasps we see holiness and righteousness uniting all that is signified by "the curtain of the tabernacle."

2) *The Measurements.* In the one "tabernacle" there were ten curtains, each twenty-eight cubits by four cubits. It is generally accepted that ten is the typical number of division. The Ten Commandments were divided into two sections: one showing our duty to God, and the other our duty to man. In the story of the ten virgins we note that five were wise and five were foolish. Ten fingers are divided by two hands; and similarly, ten toes are divided by two feet, so that, generally speaking, ten is the number of division.

Its significance in relation to this inner curtain is that it speaks of Christ in the purity of His humanity, the mystery of His divinity, the majesty of His regality, the quality of His humility, and the intensity of His severity, as the great Divider. Jesus Himself said: "Think not that I am come to send peace on earth: I came not to send peace, but a sword. For I am come to set a man at variance against his father, and the daughter against her mother, and the daughter in law against her mother in law" (Matthew 10:34-35). As He moved among men and women during His lifetime on earth, He always created a division. Time and time again we read "there was a division among the people" (John 7:43; 9:16; 10:19).

This is characteristic of every life that is full of the Holy Spirit. Either there is attraction or antagonism, but never apathy. Jesus always produced an issue; He never created a state of neutrality. His life was ever and always filled by the Holy Spirit; and perhaps this is the significance of the fifty clasps of gold, for fifty is the number of Pentecost, when the Holy Spirit was poured out. If we know a similar fullness in our lives, then we shall create division wherever we go. Men will either be attracted to Christ, or antagonized. This was so of the early Spirit-filled disciples. They either created a revival or a revolution wherever they went.

2. The Tent

"And thou shalt make curtains of goats' hair to be a covering upon the tabernacle: eleven curtains shalt thou make" (Exodus 26:7). This set of curtains was spoken of as "the tent" (Exodus 36:14-18).

a. *The Scriptural Specifications.* These curtains comprised a set of eleven, each thirty cubits long and four cubits wide; joined together by blue loops and brass clasps, making one great tent. They were made of goats' hair, and therefore their color was black. White goats are a rarity, if not completely unknown, in the east. Bedouin tents were made of goats' hair, and are described in the Song of Solomon as being black. "I am black, but comely, O ye daughters of Jerusalem, as the tents of Kedar, as the curtains of Solomon" (1:5). This tent of goats' hair completely covered the first curtain of the Tabernacle.

b. *The Spiritual Significance.* This second curtain, known as the tent, like the first, speaks of the inwardness of the Saviour's Person and work. Consider, then, first of all, the significance of:

1) *The Material.* As we have just noted, this set of curtains was made of goats' hair. Now the goat, in Scripture, is mentioned in connection with the sin offering and sinners. We read: "Take ye a kid of the goats for a sin offering" (Leviticus 9:3). "Take . . . two kids of the goats for a sin offering" on the great Day of Atonement (Leviticus 16:5-28). "One kid of the goats for a sin offering unto the LORD shall be offered" (Numbers 28:15). "He shall separate

them one from another, as a shepherd divideth his sheep from the goats" — representing the saved and the unsaved at the judgment of the nations (Matthew 25:32).

So it is fairly clear that the tent of goats' hair speaks of the Lord Jesus as the divine Sin-bearer. From the New Testament we learn that: "God sending His own Son in the likeness of sinful flesh, and for sin, condemned sin in the flesh" (Romans 8:3). Again: "Who His own self bare our sins in His own body on the tree, that we, being dead to sins, should live unto righteousness: by whose stripes ye were healed" (1 Peter 2:24). Yet again: "[God] hath made Him to be sin for us, who knew no sin; that we might be made the righteousness of God in Him" (2 Corinthians 5:21).

If we would know the true meaning of Christ's sin-bearing, we must study what happened on the Day of Atonement, as recorded in Leviticus 16. The two goats represent the death and burial of Christ. One goat was slain, and the blood sprinkled on and before the mercy seat, thus satisfying God's holy demands against a broken law. The second goat is identified with the blood of the former one, as well as the sin of the nation, and is taken away by the hand of a fit man into a land uninhabited.

Here, then, are the two aspects of Christ's sin-bearing. Jesus must die before He can bear away the sin of the world. Isaiah puts it perfectly when he says: "He hath poured out His soul unto death ... and He bare the sin of many" (53:12).

We use correct theology when we sing:

> Living, He loved me;
> Dying, He saved me;
> Buried, He carried my sins far away;
> Rising, He justified
> freely forever:

One day He's coming —
oh, glorious day!

J. Wilbur Chapman

2) *The Measurements.* In the first curtain we noticed that there were ten sets sewn together. In the second curtain we have five and six united by fifty brass clasps, attached to a hundred loops. Eleven is the number of disintegration or disorganization. When Joseph told his dream of eleven stars doing obeisance to him, he utterly disorganized his brethren (Genesis 37). When Judas betrayed his Lord, the other eleven disciples were hopelessly disorganized. After that they all forsook their Master and fled.

With that connotation, it is interesting to think of the Lord Jesus as the Sin-bearer, filled with the Holy Spirit, disintegrating the works of the devil. John in his Epistle tells us: "For this purpose the Son of God was manifested, that He might destroy the works of the devil" (1 John 3:8).

So we thank God for the rich meaning of the inner curtains of God's dwelling place.

Now let us turn to:

## II. THE OUTER COVERINGS

### (Exodus 26:14; 36:19)

These were two in number and are distinguished from the inner curtains by the term "coverings." As in the case of the curtains, we shall study them first in relation to their scriptural specifications, and then their spiritual significance.

1. The Rams' Skins

"And thou shalt make a covering for the tent of rams' skins dyed red" (Exodus 26:14). Consider first:

a. *The Scriptural Specifications.* The only specifications given relate to the materials used. There are no measurements whatsoever. It is taken for granted that the dimensions would be the same as those of the tent of goats' hair.

b. *The Spiritual Significance.* This first covering speaks of the outwardness of the Saviour's Person and work. Consider the significance of:

1) *The Material.* The ram, in this context, speaks supremely of consecration. It is true that there are other passages in the Word of God where the ram is associated with the act of substitution, as in the story of Abraham and Isaac (Genesis 22). You will remember that in the incident on Mount Moriah, "Abraham went and took the ram, and offered him up for a burnt offering in the stead of his son" (Genesis 22:13).

But in the setting of the Tabernacle it seems fairly clear that the rams' skins speak to us of Christ in His absolute consecration to God. In Leviticus 8:22,29 this animal is referred to as "the ram of consecration" (see also Exodus 29). The object of the solemn ceremony performed for Aaron and his sons was that they might be consecrated to minister to God in the priest's office (Exodus 29:35,44). How this speaks of the great High Priest, who could say, when praying for His disciples: "For their sakes I sanctify Myself, that they also might be sanctified through the truth" (John 17:19). Listen also to the words of Isaiah concerning God's Servant: "Behold My servant, whom I uphold; Mine elect [chosen], in whom My soul delighteth" (42:1). Matthew quotes the same passage when he says: "Behold My servant, whom I have chosen; My beloved, in whom My soul is well pleased: I will put My spirit upon Him, and He shall show judgment to the Gentiles" (12:18). He was chosen and anointed of God, sanctified to minister unto God in a life of priestly service.

We notice that the rams' skins were dyed red, which speaks of consecration unto death. Nothing would turn Him aside until His work on earth was completed; and even now He lives in the power of an endless life — bearing the marks in His hands, feet, and side of His love to His Master. Now He functions as a minister of the sanctuary, "a priest for ever after the order of Melchisedec" (Hebrews 7:17). As "the Son, who is consecrated for evermore," He is still ministering unto God the Father in the interests of His Church.

What a challenge this should bring to those of us who follow in His footsteps! If this is "the path the Master trod, should not the servant tread it still?" I wonder if our lives are characterized by the rams' skins dyed red?

2) *The Measurements.* As we observed in the specifications, we notice that there are no specific measurements for the rams' skins. Surely the omission of such measurements would suggest that there can be no limitations set on a life of consecrated service to God. That was certainly true in the life of our Lord Jesus Christ, and to the extent of our capabilities and capacities, it should be true of our lives.

> Love so amazing, so divine,
> Demands our souls, our lives, our all.
>
> Isaac Watts

2. The Seal Skins

"Thou shalt make a covering . . . of [seal] skins" (Exodus 26:14).

a. *The Scriptural Specifications.* As in the case of the first covering of rams' skins dyed red, so now in relation to the badgers' or seal skins there are no specifications other than reference to the materials used. There always has been discussion among scholars as to what constituted the badger skins. It is generally thought that the animal used was either a porpoise or a seal. Both of these teemed abundantly in the Nile and Red Sea, and their hides made excellent leather. The Israelites would have no trouble in obtaining large supplies before they came out of Egypt. We read: "Every man, with whom was found blue, and purple, and scarlet, and fine linen, and goats' hair, and red skins of rams, and badgers' skins, brought them" (Exodus 35:23).

The only other place where badgers' skins are mentioned, apart from the outer Tabernacle, is Ezekiel 16:10, where it says: "I . . . shod thee with badgers' skin," suggesting the idea of something coarse and durable, suitable for footwear. The color of these skins was a drab, dull, bluish grey, so that there was nothing very attractive or beautiful about the outer covering of the Tabernacle.

This second and last covering of the Tabernacle also speaks of the outwardness of the Saviour's Person and work, and has rich lessons for us to learn. Consider the significance of:

1) *The Material.* As we have seen already, the material used was that of seal skins. This was a hard, unattractive leather, calculated to resist beating rain, baking sun, or biting frost.

How this speaks of the Lord Jesus Christ in His walk of separation! With Deity veiled in such humanity as this, He made no appeal to those who lacked spiritual discernment. Isaiah could say of Him: "He hath no form nor comeliness; and when we shall see Him, there is no beauty that we should desire Him. He is despised and rejected of men; a man of sorrows, and acquainted with grief: and we hid as it were our faces from Him; He was despised, and we esteemed Him not" (53:2-3). And John tells us: "He was in the world, and the world was made by Him, and the world knew Him not. He came unto His own, and His own received Him not" (John 1:10-11).

But notwithstanding His lack of recognition, His life of separation stands out for its sheer imperviousness to attack from the world, the flesh, and the devil. So far as the world is concerned, He could say: "Be of good cheer; I have overcome the world" (John 16:33). Regarding the flesh, it is recorded that He "was in all points tempted like as we are, yet without sin" (Hebrews 4:15). With reference to the devil, He could declare: "The prince of this world cometh, and hath nothing in Me" (John 14:30). How true are the words: "[He] is holy, harmless, undefiled, separate from sinners" (Hebrews 7:26)! So He left us an example, that we should follow in His steps. Nothing less than a life of separation can ward off the evil forces of our day.

2) *The Measurements.* Once again, as in the case of the rams' skins, there are no measurements for the seal skins, suggesting that there are no limits to which we can go in our life of separation to God. The more we are separated, the more the power of God will rest upon us, and the more effective will be our witness.

So we have seen something of the wonderful teaching enshrined in the coverings of the Tabernacle. We have studied them from the innermost curtain to the outermost covering.

Adopting the reverse procedure, we can sum up the truth of these coverings by saying that they all point to Christ. The badgers' skins speak of Christ in separation; the rams' skins of Christ in His consecration; the goats' hair of Christ in His expiation; the fine twined linen of Christ in His exaltation.

Let us give thanks to God that, while unconverted people see no beauty in our Lord Jesus Christ that they might desire Him, we, as priests unto God whose eyes have been opened, can see right through the grace of His humiliation to the glory of His exaltation. May we ever see to it that our vision of Him is not dimmed, our love to Him never dissipated, and our service for Him never dilatory. He alone is worthy to receive "power, and riches, and wisdom, and strength, and honour, and glory, and blessing . . . for ever and ever. . . . Amen" (Revelation 5:12-14).

# Chapter 6

## THE FURNITURE IN THE OUTER COURT

### *Scriptures for Study*

And thou shalt make an altar of shittim wood; five cubits long, and five cubits broad; the altar shall be foursquare: and the height thereof shall be three cubits. And thou shalt make the horns of it upon the four corners thereof: his horns shall be of the same: and thou shalt overlay it with brass. And thou shalt make his pans to receive his ashes, and his shovels, and his basons, and his fleshhooks, and his firepans: all the vessels thereof thou shalt make of brass. And thou shalt make for it a grate of network of brass; and upon the net shalt thou make four brasen rings in the four corners thereof. And thou shalt put it under the compass of the altar beneath, that the net may be even to the midst of the altar. And thou shalt make staves for the altar, staves of shittim wood, and overlay them with brass. And the staves shall be put into the rings, and the staves shall be upon the two sides of the altar, to bear it. Hollow with boards shalt thou make it: as it was showed thee in the mount, so shall they make it (Exodus 27:1-8).

And he made the altar of burnt offering of shittim wood: five cubits was the length thereof, and five cubits the breadth thereof; it was foursquare; and three cubits the height thereof. And he made the horns thereof on the four corners of it; the horns thereof were of the same: and he overlaid it with brass. And he made all the vessels of the altar, the pots, and the shovels, and the basons, and the fleshhooks, and the firepans: all the vessels thereof made he of brass. And he made for the altar a brasen grate of network under the compass thereof beneath unto the midst of it. And he cast four rings for the four ends of the grate of brass, to be places for the staves (Exodus 38:1-5).

And the LORD spake unto Moses, saying, Thou shalt also make a laver of brass, and his foot also of brass, to wash withal: and thou shalt put it between the tabernacle of the congregation and the altar, and thou shalt put water therein. For Aaron and his sons shall wash their hands and their feet thereat: When they go into the tabernacle of the congregation, they shall wash with water, that they die not; or when they come near to the altar to minister, to burn offering made by fire unto the LORD: So they shall wash their hands and their feet, that they die not: and it shall be a statute for ever to them, even to him and to his seed throughout their generations (Exodus 30:17-21).

And he made the laver of brass, and the foot of it of brass, of the lookingglasses of the women assembling, which assembled at the door of the tabernacle of the congregation (Exodus 38:8).

### THE FURNITURE IN THE OUTER COURT

Scriptures for Study: Exodus 27:1-8; 38:1-5; 30:17-21; 38:8

### I. THE BRAZEN ALTAR

1. The Scriptural Specifications
   a. The Pans
   b. The Shovels
   c. The Basins
   d. The Fleshhooks
   e. The Firepans
2. The Spiritual Significance
   a. The Materials
      1) The Altar
      2) The Appurtenances
   b. The Measurements

The two pieces of furniture in the outer court of the Tabernacle were the brazen altar and the brazen laver. First of all, we shall consider these separately, and then seek to show their vital link one to the other — both in the service they rendered in the days of the Tabernacle and their meaning for us today.

## I. THE BRAZEN ALTAR

"And thou shalt make an altar of shittim wood, five cubits long, and five cubits broad; the altar shall be foursquare: and the height thereof shall be three cubits" (Exodus 27:1).

The brazen altar was the first and largest article of furniture which confronted the worshiper who entered the gate of the outer court.

1. The Scriptural Specifications

The brazen altar was in the form of a hollow box: five cubits long, five cubits broad, and three cubits high. It was without a base or a top. Most modern authorities hold the view that it was filled with earth, or possibly stones, upon which the offerings would be burned. It was made of acacia wood, overlaid with brass or copper. At each of the four corners was an ornamental horn, made of one piece with the altar.

The position and function of the grate of network, mentioned in Exodus 27:4-5 is most obscure and uncertain. In all probability, it was a form of protection for the sides of the altar from the feet of the ministering priests, as well as the animals which were tied to the horns of the altar before being slain.

The "compass" of the altar was a projecting shelf, or ledge, halfway between the top and the base of the altar, supported all around its outer edge by the vertical netlike grating of bronze that rested on the ground. Its purpose was either to catch any portions of the sacrifices which might have fallen accidentally from the altar, or to enable the priests to carry on their work conveniently on the top of the altar. This latter suggestion may explain Leviticus 9:22, where Aaron is said to have come "down from" the altar. The ledge also would have been used to hold some of the utensils which were used directly in the manipulating of the sacrifices.

At each corner of the bronze gate were rings, through which the two staves were passed, for the carrying of the altar when on the march.

Associated with the altar were five utensils:

a. *The Pans,* used for carrying the ashes from the altar to a prescribed place outside the camp.

b. *The Shovels,* used for picking up ashes, and for feeding the fire.

c. *The Basins,* used for holding the blood of victims,

which was sometimes carried inside, and more often poured out at the foot of the altar.

d. *The Fleshhooks,* used for adjusting the pieces of the victim upon the wood. They were three-pronged instruments (see 1 Samuel 2:13).

e. *The Firepans,* or censers, used for carrying burning embers from the brazen altar to the altar of incense. In all probability, this is why they are called censers.

When journeying, it was particularly specified that the altar should be draped first with a purple covering and then with a second covering of badgers' skins (see Numbers 4:13-14). This was the only piece of furniture which was carried in the royal color.

2. The Spiritual Significance

The brazen altar is full of rich symbolism and spiritual instruction. Let us, then, consider the significance of:

a. *The Materials.* These include the altar and the appurtenances.

1) *The Altar.* "And thou shalt make an altar of shittim wood . . . and thou shalt overlay it with brass" (Exodus 27:1,2).

The *acacia wood,* once again, speaks of our Lord's holy and incorruptible humanity. He was the "holy thing" conceived of the Holy Ghost, born of Mary, called the Son of God (see Luke 1:35).

The *brass* speaks of His divine righteousness expressed in human life, and enduring suffering even unto death. So it is recorded that Jesus "endured the cross, despising the shame" (Hebrews 12:2).

The *wood* overlaid with brass constituted a fireproof combination. Only comparatively recently has it been discovered by scientists what an ingenious, fire-resisting invention is hard wood overlaid with copper and hermetically sealed. How wonderfully this combination speaks of the Person of our Lord Jesus Christ, who endured the fires of Calvary without being consumed; like the bush which Moses saw in the wilderness which burned with fire but was not destroyed (Exodus 3:1-5). Peter, quoting from Psalm 16, expresses this plainly in his Pentecostal sermon when he declares: "Thou wilt not . . . suffer thine Holy One to see corruption" (Acts 2:27).

One piece with the altar were the *four horns.* The horn in Scripture is always a symbol of strength, salvation, and security. When Hannah rejoiced over the victory of God in her life, she exclaimed, "The LORD . . . shall give strength unto His king, and exalt the horn of His anointed" (1 Samuel 2:10). The Lord Jesus is described in Revelation 5:6 as "a Lamb as it had been slain, having seven horns." So the horns on the altar speak of the victory of the cross and the saving power of the gospel. Through His cross, the Son of God "spoiled principalities and powers, [and] made a show of them openly, triumphing over them" (Colossians 2:15). The great apostle, anticipating evangelistic crusades in the proud and powerful city of Rome, says: "I am not ashamed of the gospel of Christ: for it is the power of God unto salvation to every one that believeth" (Romans 1:16).

As well as being the symbol of *strength* and *salvation,* the horns also speak of *security.* The Psalmist speaks of binding the sacrifice to the horns of the altar (Psalm 118:27). The blood of the sin offering was smeared on these horns (Exodus 29:19; Leviticus 4:7; 8:15; 9:9; 16:18). Thus, to have laid hold of the horns was an emphatic mode of laying claim to the right of the sanctuary. So we read: "If a man come presumptuously upon his neighbour, to slay him with guile; thou shalt take him from Mine altar, that he may die" (Exodus 21:14). Instances occur in Scripture of those who sought refuge by taking hold of the horns of the altar. There was Adonijah who "feared because of Solomon, and arose, and went, and caught hold on the horns of the altar" (1 Kings 1:50). There was Joab, who "fled unto the tabernacle of the LORD, and caught hold on the horns of the altar" (1 Kings 2:28-29).

The *grate of network,* as we have seen, appears to have been a protection for the altar against the feet of the ministering priests, and particularly the sacrificial animals that were tied before being slain. If this view of the grate is correct, then surely the network of brass speaks of God's principle of righteousness and justice which protects the gospel of the cross from all who kick against the blood and attempt to deny its efficacy. Writing to the Romans, Paul says: "Being justified freely by His grace through the redemption that is in Christ Jesus: Whom God hath set forth to be a propitiation through faith in His blood, to declare His righteousness for the remission of sins that are past, through the forbearance of God; To declare, I say, at this time His righteousness: that He might be just, and the justifier of him which believeth in Jesus" (3:24-26).

The *rings* and *staves* for carrying the altar also have a message for us. There were two staves, speaking of the two aspects of the gospel: namely, His death and resurrection. "Christ died for our sins according to the scriptures; . . . He was buried, and . . . rose again the third day according to the scriptures" (1 Corinthians 15:3-4). The rings and staves made the altar portable, and so suggest that the message of the cross is for all the world. Jesus said: "Go ye into all the world, and preach the gospel to every creature" (Mark 16:15).

Thus we see that the brazen altar in its various aspects speaks of the Lord Jesus as the conquering Christ of Calvary.

2) *The Appurtenances.* "And thou shalt make his pans to receive his ashes, and his shovels, and his basons, and his

fleshhooks, and his firepans: all the vessels thereof thou shalt make of brass" (Exodus 27:3). These five utensils were all made of brass or copper, and so speak of the divine righteousness of our Lord Jesus Christ worked out in obedience unto death.

The *pans* suggest the *thoroughness* of the Saviour's cross work. They were used for the ashes, which speak of the completed sacrifice. The Lord Jesus was never satisfied with the work which God gave Him to do until He could cry: "It is finished" (John 19:30). His constant ambition was expressed thus: "My meat is to do the will of Him that sent Me, and to finish His work" (John 4:34).

The *shovels* suggest the *faithfulness* of the Saviour's cross work. These were used for picking up the ashes — and particularly for tending or feeding the fire. There was never an instance in the life of Christ when He avoided the cost of the cross. We read that He "endured the cross, despising the shame" (Hebrews 12:2). Again: "Though He were a Son, yet learned He obedience by the things which He suffered" (Hebrews 5:8). And again: "He . . . became obedient unto death, even the death of the cross" (Philippians 2:8).

The *basins* suggest the *selflessness* of the Saviour's cross work. They held the blood of the sacrifices, which was carried inside, or more often poured out at the foot of the altar. What selflessness characterized the life of the Son of God! He emptied Himself of His heavenly glory in order to become our Saviour. We read that "though He was rich, yet for [our] sake He became poor, that [we] through His poverty might be rich" (2 Corinthians 8:9).

The *fleshhooks* suggest the *steadfastness* of the Saviour's cross work. These were three-pronged instruments for arranging the sacrifice in order upon the wood. If and when the sacrifice moved from its place, it was deliberately brought back to the center of the flame with the use of the fleshhook.

Even in His lifetime the Lord Jesus steadfastly set His face to go to Jerusalem, and to the cross. But perhaps the fleshhook was more particularly applied when He hung on the cross and listened to the taunts of those who said: "If Thou be Christ, save Thyself and us" (Luke 23:39). The application of the fleshhook involved Him in self-imposed weakness in order that He might become your Saviour and mine. So Paul tells us: "Though He was crucified through weakness, yet He liveth by the power of God" (2 Corinthians 13:4).

The *firepans* suggest the *zealousness* of the Saviour's cross work. These censers were employed to carry the burning embers from the brazen altar to the altar of incense. Although the fire on the altar speaks of the wrath of God against sin, it also signifies the zeal, passion, and love which burned in the Saviour's heart to deal with the matter of sin, and to accomplish man's redemption. During the days of His flesh that zeal revealed itself in His holy jealousy for the sanctity of God's house; and His disciples remembered that it was written, "The zeal of Thine house hath eaten Me up" (John 2:17). On the cross that flame of zeal burned at its fiercest, until the sacrifice was complete. Only living coals from off that altar can set alight the altars of our hearts. We capture the zeal of our Saviour from the censers associated with the altar of burnt offering. The fire from Heaven that burned on the brazen altar never went out. In Leviticus 6:13 we read: "The fire shall ever be burning upon the altar; it shall never go out."

With these materials of the altar, we now turn to:

b. *The Measurements.* "And thou shalt make an altar of shittim wood, five cubits long, and five cubits broad; the altar shall be foursquare: and the height thereof shall be three cubits" (Exodus 27:1). As already pointed out, it was the largest article of furniture. Some believe that it was big enough to hold every other piece of furniture in the Tabernacle.

This in itself is most suggestive. Only through the cross of our Lord Jesus Christ can we understand and enjoy the many other blessings that accompany salvation. "Five cubits, four-square" suggests the universal appeal of the grace of God manifested through the cross. Five is the number of grace, while four speaks of universality. How true are the words of the Lord Jesus when He said: "I, if I be lifted up from the earth, will draw all men unto Me" (John 12:32). In the "three cubits high" there is a hint of the third day, when our great and sufficient Sacrifice was accepted by a satisfied God, who raised Him from the dead for our justification.

One more thought remains to be considered in connection with the spiritual significance of the altar:

c. *The Ministry*. In general terms, the brazen altar represented a twofold ministry:

1) *The Ministry of Expiation*. In Hebrews 5:1 we are told that the high priest is "ordained . . . that he may offer both gifts and sacrifices for sins." The gifts we shall consider in a moment. The sacrifices constituted the expiatory offerings. Among the five offerings mentioned in the first five chapters of Leviticus, the two that are related to the ministry of expiation are the sin offering and the trespass offering. They made atonement or reconciliation for those on whose behalf they were presented. So we read that "without shedding of blood is no remission" (Hebrews 9:22).

This ministry of expiation was wonderfully carried out by our Lord Jesus Christ, in whom the high priest, the sacrifice, and the altar all find their fulfillment. So the Apostle Paul tells us: "God . . . hath reconciled us to Himself by Jesus Christ. . . . For He hath made Him to be sin for us, who knew no sin; that we might be made the righteousness of God in Him" (2 Corinthians 5:18,21).

Thus we see that the altar first of all speaks of the ministry of expiation; and also of:

2) *The Ministry of Consecration.* The high priest is "ordained . . . that he may offer both gifts and sacrifices" (Hebrews 5:1). The gifts represent the dedicatory offerings. Such a gift might be a bloodless offering, as in the case of the meal offering. On the other hand, it included also the burnt offering and the peace offering. While there is an expiatory aspect of the burnt offering, the main idea in this offering was that of a life devoted or dedicated to God. It was a recognition of, and response to, God's claim upon the individual.

In this respect, our Lord Jesus Christ completely fulfills the type. He was a perfect sin offering, the Lamb of God without blemish, because of His utter consecration to the will of God. He was an offering of "a sweetsmelling savour" unto God (Ephesians 5:2), who could say of Him: "This is My beloved Son, in whom I am well pleased" (Matthew 3:17).

We can have no share in the mysterious expiatory offering of Christ, for it was a work peculiar to Himself; but there is a sense in which we can follow our Lord in the dedicatory offering, so that the apostle exhorts us: "By the mercies of God . . . present your bodies a living sacrifice, holy, acceptable unto God, which is your reasonable service" (Romans 12:1).

Let us now consider:

## II. THE BRAZEN LAVER

### (Exodus 30:17-21; 38:8; 40:7)

"And the LORD spake unto Moses, saying, Thou shalt also make a laver of brass, and his foot also of brass, to wash withal: and thou shalt put it between the tabernacle of the congregation and the altar, and thou shalt put water therein" (Exodus 30:17-18).

The brazen laver constituted the second piece of furniture in the outer court of the Tabernacle. It stood between the altar and the door of the Tabernacle.

## 1. The Scriptural Specifications

The brazen laver and its foot were to be made out of the mirrors of the women who assembled at the door of the congregation (Exodus 38:8). These women seem to have voluntarily given up these articles of luxury for this purpose. Highly polished copper mirrors were much used by the ancient Egyptians, and the women of Israel must have brought out with them great quantities of these looking glasses.

It is interesting to note that there are no specifications as to size or shape of this laver. The brazen sea and ten lavers that served the same purpose in the Temple of Solomon were elaborately made with exquisite designs, which are minutely described in 1 Kings 7:23-29. The late John Kitto held the view that the laver, whatever its shape, stood upon another basin, more wide and shallow, as a cup and saucer; and the latter received from cocks or spouts in the upper basin the water which was allowed to escape. The priests washed themselves with the water that fell from the upper basin. If by the underbasin we understand the *foot* of the laver, then the sense is clear. The text does say that the priests were to wash themselves *at* the laver, and not *in* the laver.

## 2. The Spiritual Significance

The laver, like the brazen altar, is full of rich teaching. Observe the significance of:

a. *The Materials.* As we have noted in the specifications, the laver was made of bronze, or polished copper, looking glasses provided by the women who assembled at the door of the Tabernacle (Exodus 38:8). Once again, the brass speaks of the divine righteousness of the Lord Jesus, expressed in human life and enduring suffering unto death. In the provision of this material by the women of Israel, we see self-judgment on that which speaks of outward adornment. When we are confronted with the righteousness of the Lord Jesus, as expressed in His cross work, we cannot fashion ourselves according to the course of this world. If truly yielded to God, we must not be "conformed to this world: but . . . transformed by the renewing of [our] mind" (Romans 12:2). It was to women who knew something of self-judgment and surrender through the cross that Paul wrote: "In like manner also, that [the] women adorn themselves in modest apparel, with shamefacedness and sobriety; not with broided hair, or gold, or pearls, or costly array; But (which becometh women professing godliness) with good works" (1 Timothy 2:9-10). Then there was a similar word from Peter to women, saying: "Whose adorning, let it not be that outward adorning of plaiting the hair, and of wearing of gold, or of putting on of apparel; But let it be the hidden man of the heart, in that which is not corruptible, even the ornament of a meek and quiet spirit, which is in the sight of God of great price" (1 Peter 3:3-4). Needless to say, the same principles apply to men!

The brazen laver contained water which, without doubt, speaks of the Spirit of God, operating through the Word of God. We read that the Lord Jesus "loved the church, and gave Himself for it; That He might sanctify and cleanse it with the washing of water by the word" (Ephesians 5:25-26). The Word only convicts and cleanses in the measure in which the Holy Spirit interprets and applies it, for "the letter killeth, but the spirit giveth life" (2 Corinthians 3:6). Jesus said: "The words that I speak unto you, they are spirit, and they are life" (John 6:63).

b. *The Measurements.* As we have seen, there are no dimensions given for this article of furniture. Such omissions — as indeed additions and variations — in Scripture are always highly significant. Undoubtedly, the suggestion in this omission of measurements is that the laver was limitless in its application. As we shall see in a moment, the priests were constantly having to wash at the laver, if their service was to be acceptable to God. Indeed, not to wash was to die.

Under this heading of "measurements" we do well to recognize also the significant positioning of the laver. It followed the altar and yet was dependent upon the altar. Like all other articles of furniture, it was sprinkled with the blood of atonement. We read that Moses sprinkled "with blood both the tabernacle, and all the vessels of the ministry. And almost all things are by the law purged with blood" (Hebrews 9:21-22). The laver could not be used until after the blood had been shed. The Spirit cannot operate through the Word without the foundation work of the cross. When Christ entered into Heaven by His own blood, He sent the Holy Spirit to convict the world of sin, of righteousness, and of judgment. There is a sense, then, in which the altar speaks of Calvary, while the laver speaks of Pentecost.

c. *The Ministry.* While the altar speaks of the ministry of reconciliation, the laver speaks of the ministry of separation, or sanctification. There are two aspects of this sanctifying work:

1) *The Initial Cleansing.* When the priests were inducted to their high and holy office, they were bathed all over at the laver. Moses was to bring Aaron and his sons to the door of the Tabernacle of the congregation and wash them with water (Exodus 29:4). The only other occasion when anyone was bathed completely was on the Day of Atonement (Leviticus 16:4), which represented a new beginning each year for the whole nation.

The initial cleansing answers to *regeneration* by the Spirit, through the Word. It is an experience which is never repeated. Paul refers to it in Titus 3:5 when he says: "Not by works of righteousness which we have done, but according to His mercy He saved us, by the washing of regeneration, and renewing of the Holy Ghost." Our Lord also spoke of it on the occasion when He washed the disciples' feet, saying to Peter: "He that is washed [completely washed] needeth not save to wash [partially wash] his feet, but is clean every whit" (John 13:10).

With the initial cleansing, there is also:

2) *The Continual Cleansing.* The word for the priests was: "When they go into the tabernacle of the congregation, they shall wash with water, that they die not; or when they come near to the altar to minister, to burn offering made by fire unto the LORD: So they shall wash their hands and their feet, that they die not" (Exodus 30:20-21).

Here is solemn instruction. These priests dare not touch either the altar or the Tabernacle without washing, lest they die. The reason for this was that they were in constant contact with defilement. Remember that there was no floor, either in the outer court or the Tabernacle. They were never allowed to sit down, so that in moving about they were unavoidably brought into contact with the dust of the desert; and yet they knew all the time that God's unalterable demand was: "be ye clean, that bear the vessels of the LORD" (Isaiah 52:11). So hands and feet were washed continually at the brazen laver; hands speaking of their *work,* and feet suggesting their *walk.*

The application of this Old Testament typology is equally serious and solemn. God will not allow us to touch His work without being clean. Paul tells us: "They that are in the flesh cannot please God. . . . If ye live after the flesh, ye shall die: but if ye through the Spirit do mortify the deeds of the body, ye shall live" (Romans 8:8,13).

Perhaps the fact that we are so dead and ineffective in relation to our worship and witness is because we are defiled Christians. To continue in such defilement merits a physical cutting off, for John warns us, "There is a sin unto death: I do not say that [ye] shall pray for it" (1 John 5:16). How necessary, then, to maintain daily cleansing! Jesus said: "He that is washed needeth not save to wash his feet, but is clean every whit" (John 13:10).

The Old Testament priests had to wash hands and feet because their life depended upon the works of the law. Believers under grace wash only their feet; and if our walk is right with God then what we do is blessed of God. This daily cleansing is the application of the Word of God to our hearts and lives by the power of the Holy Spirit. "Wherewithal shall a young man cleanse his way?" The answer is, "by taking heed thereto according to Thy word" (Psalm 119:9). Speaking to His disciples, Jesus said: "Now ye are clean through the word which I have spoken unto you" (John 15:3). Later, praying for them, He said: "Sanctify them through Thy truth: Thy word is truth" (John 17:17). Paul reminds us that the Lord Jesus is constantly sanctifying and cleansing the Church "with the washing of water by the word" (Ephesians 5:26). How important, then, that we should daily and hourly apply the Word of God, by the power of the Spirit, to our lives. Let us never forget that even the food we eat and all things are "sanctified by the word of God and prayer" (1 Timothy 4:5).

What rich and yet challenging lessons emerge from the study of these two articles of furniture in the outer court. The brazen altar teaches us the way of reconciliation, while the brazen laver leads us into the way of sanctification. Without reconciliation we can never know sanctification. But if we are truly reconciled to God then let us see to it that we know both positional and practical sanctification. Positional sanctification is the once-for-all washing of regeneration by the Word that establishes the indissoluble relationship. Practical sanctification is the day-by-day and moment-by-moment cleansing by the Word through the Spirit. Without this practical sanctification there is no fellowship with God, and worship and witness become ineffective and barren.

God's words to His ancient people, and to His Church today, are: "Ye shall be holy: for I the LORD your God am holy" (Leviticus 19:2).

Let us never forget that without holiness there is no happiness. May God, therefore, make us a truly holy people.

# Chapter 7

## THE FURNITURE IN THE HOLY PLACE

### *Scriptures for Study*

Thou shalt also make a table of shittim wood: two cubits shall be the length thereof, and a cubit the breadth thereof, and a cubit and a half the height thereof. And thou shalt overlay it with pure gold, and make thereto a crown of gold round about. And thou shalt make unto it a border of a hand breadth round about, and thou shalt make a golden crown to the border thereof round about. And thou shalt make for it four rings of gold, and put the rings in the four corners that are on the four feet thereof. Over against the border shall the rings be for places of the staves to bear the table. And thou shalt make the staves of shittim wood, and overlay them with gold, that the table may be borne with them. And thou shalt make the dishes thereof, and spoons thereof, and covers thereof, and bowls thereof, to cover withal: of pure gold shalt thou make them. And thou shalt set upon the table showbread before Me alway.

And thou shalt make a candlestick of pure gold: of beaten work shall the candlestick be made: his shaft, and his branches, his bowls, his knops, and his flowers, shall be of the same. And six branches shall come out of the sides of it; three branches of the candlestick out of the one side, and three branches of the candlestick out of the other side: Three bowls made like unto almonds, with a knop and a flower in one branch; and three bowls made like almonds in the other branch, with a knop and a flower: so in the six branches that come out of the candlestick. And in the candlestick shall be four bowls made like unto almonds, with their knops and their flowers. And there shall be a knop under two branches of the same, and a knop under two branches of the same, and a knop under two branches of the same, according to the six branches that proceed out of the candlestick. Their knops and their branches shall be of the same: all [of] it shall be one beaten work of pure gold. And thou shalt make the seven lamps thereof: and they shall light the lamps thereof, that they may give light over against it. And the tongs thereof, and the snuffdishes thereof, shall be of pure gold. Of a talent of pure gold shall he make it, with all these vessels. And look that thou make them after their pattern, which was showed thee in the mount (Exodus 25:23-40; see also Exodus 30:1-10,34-38; 31:8; 37:10-28; 39:37; Leviticus 24:5-9; Hebrews 9:2).

## THE FURNITURE IN THE HOLY PLACE

Scriptures for Study: Exodus 25:23-40; 30:1-10,34-38; 31:8; 37:10-28; 39:37; Leviticus 24:5-9; Hebrews 9:2

### I.  THE GOLDEN CANDLESTICK

1. The Scriptural Specifications

2. The Spiritual Significance
    a. The Materials
        1) The Composition of the Lampstand
        2) The Decoration of the Lampstand
        3) The Illumination of the Lampstand
        4) The Supervision of the Lampstand
    b. The Measurements
    c. The Ministry
        1) The Light of Attraction
        2) The Light of Perception

## II.  THE TABLE OF SHOWBREAD

1. The Scriptural Specifications

2. The Spiritual Significance
   a. The Materials
      1) The Table
      2) The Showbread
      3) The Vessels
   b. The Measurements
   c. The Ministry
      1) The Food
      2) Fellowship

## III.  THE ALTAR OF INCENSE

1. The Scriptural Specifications

2. The Spiritual Significance
   a. The Materials
      1) The Altar
      2) The Incense
   b. The Measurements
   c. The Ministry
      1) Adoration
      2) Intercession

The three pieces of furniture in the holy place of the Tabernacle were the golden candlestick, the table of showbread, and the altar of incense. As in our last study, we shall consider these separately, and then seek to show their vital link one to the other, both in the service they rendered in the days of the Tabernacle and their meaning for us today.

## I. THE GOLDEN CANDLESTICK

### (Exodus 25:31-40; 37:17-24; 39:37)

"And thou shalt make a candlestick of pure gold: of beaten work shall the candlestick be made: his shaft, and his branches, his bowls, his knops, and his flowers, shall be of the same. . . . And look that thou make them after their pattern, which was showed thee in the mount" (Exodus 25:31,40).

The golden candlestick would be the first piece of furniture to engage the attention of the worshiper as he entered the door of the Tabernacle into the holy place. With its seven lights burning brightly, it would present an attractive object of golden splendor. Let us draw near and examine it.

1. The Scriptural Specifications

The golden candlestick consisted of a central stem (called "the candlestick" — Exodus 25:34; or "his shaft" — Exodus 25:31, with three branches at each side of it — Exodus 25:32). The lamps, with their wicks and oil, were set on the stem and its six branches. Each branch was intricately wrought with the likeness of almond blossoms, pomegranates (or knops), and lilies. There were three of these ornaments on each branch, and four on the central shaft (Exodus 25:33-34). The ornaments were of one piece with the whole candlestick (Exodus 25:36).

Associated with the golden candlestick were the tongs, to trim the wick; and the snuff dishes, to hold the trimmings (Exodus 25:38). The lamps were to be fed with pure olive oil (Exodus 27:20; 39:27).

2. The Spiritual Significance

To be as comprehensive as possible, we shall consider the spiritual significance of each of the articles of furniture in the holy place, in terms of the materials, the measurements, and the ministry.

a. *The Materials.* The candlestick and its adjuncts were all of pure gold. They consisted of the lampstand, the lamps (which contained the oil and wicks), the tongs, and the snuff dishes. Each piece is instinct with valuable spiritual lessons.

*The Lampstand.* "And thou shalt make a candlestick of pure gold: of beaten work shall the candlestick be made: his shaft, and his branches, his bowls, his knops, and his flowers, shall be of the same. . . . And thou shalt make the seven lamps thereof: and they shall light the lamps thereof, that they may give light over against it. And the tongs thereof, and the snuffdishes thereof, shall be of pure gold" (Exodus 25:31,37-38).

We have here four main considerations:

1) *The Composition of the Lampstand.* The basic composition of the lampstand is described as "his shaft, and his branches" (Exodus 25:31). C. W. Slemming points out that the Hebrew word translated "shaft" means "thigh," "loins," or even "body" (see Genesis 46:26; Exodus 1:5; etc.). Here is a precious thought indeed! Christ is the Shaft, out of whom we — the branches — have been made. Just as Eve was taken out of Adam's side, so the Church has come into being through the piercing of the Saviour's body. We read that the candlestick was to be of "one beaten work of pure gold" (Exodus 25:36). It was through the beating that the shaft was made of one piece with the branches.

We know that it was through the wounding and bruising at Calvary that the union between Christ and His Church was established. Isaiah tells us that "He was wounded for our transgressions, He was bruised for our iniquities: the chastisement of our peace was upon Him; and with His stripes we are healed" (53:5). Again: "It pleased the LORD to bruise Him; He hath put Him to grief: when thou shalt make His soul an offering for sin, *He shall see His seed*" (53:10).

Paul tells us that "Christ . . . loved the church, and gave

Himself for it." Because of such self-giving, "we are members of His body, of His flesh, and of His bones" (Ephesians 5:25,30). The writer to the Hebrews expresses the same thought: "It became Him, for whom are all things, and by whom are all things, in bringing many sons unto glory, to make the captain of their salvation perfect through sufferings. For both He that sanctifieth and they who are sanctified are all of one: for which cause He is not ashamed to call them brethren" (2:10-11).

How wonderful to know that by virtue of the cross work and through faith in Him we are "partakers of the divine nature" (2 Peter 1:4), and therefore "one piece of pure gold" with our risen Head. Let it be added, however, that though we are one with Him, He ever and only must have the pre-eminence as the Head of the Church (Colossians 1:18). This is significantly suggested by the prominence of the central shaft of the candlestick.

2) *The Decoration of the Lampstand.* This sevenfold candelabra was wrought in bowls, knops, and flowers (Exodus 25:31). It is generally accepted that the bowls were almonds, while the knops represented pomegranates, and the flowers were lilies.

The *lilies* speak of Christ in His life of purity. The Song of Solomon speaks of our Lord as "the lily of the valleys" (2:1) and, as such, He was "holy, harmless, undefiled, separate from sinners" (Hebrews 7:26).

The *pomegranates* speak of Christ in His life of productiveness. The pomegranate is the emblem of fruitfulness. It was seen on the hem of the high priest's garment, in the decorations of Solomon's Temple, and in the garden of fruitfulness in the Song of Solomon (7:12). Jesus could say to His disciples: "He that abideth in Me, and I in him, the same bringeth forth much fruit: for without Me ye can do nothing" (John 15:5; see also verses 8,16).

The *almonds* speak of Christ in His life of power. Almond blossoms symbolize resurrection. We recall how Aaron's rod budded, blossomed, and bare almonds overnight, thus typifying our Lord in His resurrection (see Numbers 17:8). Paul longed to know this resurrection power. His ambition is expressed in those familiar words of Philippians 3:10: "That I may know Him, and the power of His resurrection, and the fellowship of His sufferings, being made conformable unto His death."

It is interesting to note that these ornaments appeared three times on the branches and four times on the shaft. Three times on the branches speaks of our completeness in Christ, in His purity, productiveness, and power; four times on the main shaft marks Christ off as distinctive from us, as the One who appeals universally in terms of His life of purity, peace, and power.

3) *The Illumination of the Lampstand.* The seven lamps which stood on the shaft and branches of the lampstand were probably like those used by the Egyptians and other nations: usually a shallow covered vessel, more or less of oval form, with a mouth at one end from which the wick protruded.

It seems fairly evident that the central lamp speaks of Christ as the Light of the world. He could say: "I am the light of the world: he that followeth Me shall not walk in darkness, but shall have the light of life" (John 8:12).

The six other lamps represent His believing people. Of them the Lord Jesus could say, "Ye are the light of the world" (Matthew 5:14); and again: "Let your light so shine before men, that they may see your good works, and glorify your Father which is in heaven" (Matthew 5:16). Paul exhorts the saints at Philippi to "shine as lights in the world" (Philippians 2:15).

The lamps were fed with "golden oil," or pure oil of olives (Exodus 27:20). Oil, as we know, is a symbol of the

Holy Spirit, who is spoken of in the New Testament as "the anointing" (1 John 2:27). In our lives, as in the life of the Lord Jesus Christ, we are utterly dependent upon the Holy Spirit for maintaining the spiritual glow.

The *wicks* quite obviously represent the human life, and how comforting to know that however weak our wicks may be, a "smoking flax will He not quench" (Matthew 12:20). Our ambition should be ever to burn out for God, even as did our Saviour.

4) *The Supervision of the Lampstand.* The priests were responsible for cleaning, replenishing, and lighting the lamps each morning and evening, for the lamps were to "burn always" (Exodus 27:20), or "burn continually" (Leviticus 24:2). To maintain this "clear, pure light," the priests had to use two accessories, namely, the tongs and the snuff dishes. The tongs were for trimming the wicks, and the snuff dishes were for carrying the trimmings away.

In the life of the Lord Jesus, the tongs and snuff dishes represented self-discipline and obedience to His heavenly Father. We read, "Though He were a Son, yet learned He obedience by the things which He suffered" (Hebrews 5:8). A similar discipline is needed in our own lives, if we would burn brightly for God. If and when there is a refusal to do this, then God has to do the chastening, for "whom the Lord loveth He chasteneth" (Hebrews 12:6). If there is willful resistance after this, then the word which inevitably comes is "repent . . . or else I will . . . remove thy candlestick out of his place, except thou repent" (Revelation 2:5).

b. *The Measurements.* Although it has been estimated that its height may have been about three feet and its width two feet, there are actually no scriptural specifications as to its size. This very omission — as in the case of the laver — shows the limitlessness of its influence.

The weight of the candlestick was one talent, which is

equal to about one hundred twenty-five pounds (Exodus 25:39). It has been estimated that its value as gold then was about eighteen thousand dollars, or about fifty thousand dollars today. This estimate, of course, does not include the cost of the hours of intricate work put into it.

As we have observed, the candlestick was of one single piece of solid gold, speaking of Christ in the glory of His divine nature, first of all; and then, secondly, of His believing people who have been made partakers of the same divine nature. The candlestick stood on the south side of the holy place, thus directly casting its light across to the table of showbread on the north side.

c. *The Ministry.* The instructions were that the priests were to light the lamps that they might give light over against it (Exodus 25:37). Again we read that when the Tabernacle was first erected, Moses "lighted the lamps before the LORD" (Exodus 40:25). Through these two passages we learn that the ministry of the candlestick was twofold. It provided:

1) *The Light of Attraction.* "They shall light the lamps thereof, that they may give light over against it" (Exodus 25:37). The light of the lamps drew attraction to the glory of the candlestick. A German writer of great insight once said that "Jesus Christ knew no greater task than to attract men and women to Himself." Jesus said: "I am the light of the world: he that followeth Me shall not walk in darkness" (John 8:12). We, too, as followers of Christ, have no greater privilege than to attract people to Christ with the very light that we have been divinely given. So it behooves us to have our loins girded about, and our lights burning (Luke 12:35).

2) *The Light of Perception.* Moses "lighted the lamps before the LORD" (Exodus 40:25). In the holy place the glow of the lamps enabled the priests, in the presence of God, to worship and serve intelligently. There is a tremendous

word which David uses in Psalm 36:9, "In Thy light shall we see light." Whether it is direct light from Christ, or diffused light through the Christian, all light is given us for perception. In His light shall we see light.

So we are led to see deeper meaning in the table of showbread, which speaks of fellowship and satisfaction. "If we walk in the light, as He is in the light, we have fellowship one with another, and the blood of Jesus Christ His Son cleanseth us from all sin" (1 John 1:7). In His light also we are attracted to perceive deeper meaning in the altar of incense, which speaks of adoration and intercession. "We know not what we should pray for as we ought: but the Spirit [Himself] maketh intercession for us with groanings which cannot be uttered. And He that searcheth the hearts knoweth what is the mind of the Spirit, because He maketh intercession for the saints according to the will of God" (Romans 8:26-27).

How we praise God for this twofold ministry of the candlestick! Let us remember that "he that doeth truth cometh to the light, that his deeds may be . . . manifest, that they are wrought in God" (John 3:21).

Let us now consider:

## II.  THE TABLE OF SHOWBREAD

### (Exodus 25:23-30; 31:8; 37:10-16; Leviticus 24:5-9; Hebrews 9:2)

On the inner side of the holy place stood the table of showbread with its twelve loaves of bread. There is something very appealing about this article of furniture, for it represents fellowship and satisfaction. First of all, however, let us observe:

1. The Scriptural Specifications

The table was made of shittim wood, two cubits in length, one cubit in breadth, and one-and-a-half cubits in height, overlaid with pure gold and having a golden crown to the border thereof round about (Exodus 25:24). Just below the top of the table was a border of about four-and-a-half inches, which encircled the table to keep it firm. This border also had a ridge like a golden crown. It is difficult to determine from the text whether this second crowned border was on the same level as the table surface, or lower, as some suggest. Its purpose, no doubt, was to contain the various utensils that were used in connection with the ministry of the table of showbread. Within the first border were contained the twelve cakes, or loaves, of showbread. The bread, in all probability, was placed on twelve golden dishes. On each loaf was a golden censer, or saucer, containing frankincense, which when fired smoked continuously.

Then there were jugs, or cups, of pure gold, that probably were used for the drink offering. Other utensils were the spoons, used for putting the incense on the bread. Attached to the four legs of the table were rings, to take two staves for bearing the table when the camp was on the march.

2. The Spiritual Significance

In the table of showbread we have, once again, precious truths that are symbolized in the materials, measurements, and ministry.

a. *The Materials.* There are three main aspects to which I would draw your attention: the table, the showbread, and the vessels.

1) *The Table.* "Thou shalt also make a table of shittim wood. . . . And thou shalt overlay it with pure gold" (Exodus 25:23-24). We are familiar with this symbolism. Here is our Lord Jesus Christ seen once again in His perfect divinity and humanity. The table, resting on four legs, suggests the Lord

Jesus in His risen glory. The two crowns are suggestive of Him crowned: with thorns on the cross, and then with glory on the throne. There are others who hold the view that the two crowns represent His twofold Headship: first, as Head of all the Church, and then one day as Head of all creation. Paul tells us in Colossians 1:18 that "He is the head of the body, the church" (see also Ephesians 5:23). Then there is coming a day when we shall see all things in subjection under His feet. For this purpose "God . . . hath highly exalted Him, and given Him a name which is above every name: That at the name of Jesus every knee should bow, of things in heaven, and things in earth, and things under the earth; And that every tongue should confess that Jesus Christ is Lord, to the glory of God the Father" (Philippians 2:9-11).

The rings and staves speak of our Lord Jesus Christ in His perpetual and personal presence with us. The rings speak of His perpetuity, while the staves denote His mobility and intimacy. He said: "Lo, I am with you alway, even unto the end of the [age] " (Matthew 28:20). Again we read: "He hath said, I will never leave thee, nor forsake thee" (Hebrews 13:5). How wonderful to know that our risen Lord, crowned with glory and honor, is ever with us to feed our hungry souls with the living bread!

2) *The Showbread.* "And thou shalt set upon the table showbread before Me alway" (Exodus 25:30). Showbread literally means "the bread of the faces." It was also called "the bread of the presence" (Leviticus 24:8), the "perpetual bread" (Numbers 4:7), and "holy bread" (1 Samuel 21:4-6). It is not difficult to interpret the meaning of the showbread in the light of the New Testament. Jesus is our living Bread, come down from Heaven, ministered to us through the Word, by the power of the Holy Spirit. When Jesus spoke of this Bread, He called it "the bread of truth," "the bread of God," and "the bread of life" (see John 6:32,33,35). No wonder

the disciples later prayed, "Lord, evermore give us this bread" (John 6:34).

3) *The Vessels.* "Thou shalt make the dishes thereof, and spoons thereof, and covers thereof, and bowls thereof, to cover withal: of pure gold shalt thou make them" (Exodus 25:29). The dishes, or chargers, were used for conveying the bread into the sanctuary; or alternatively, might have been employed for carrying the fine flour which formed part of the offering of the princes of Israel (see Numbers 7:13).

*The spoons* were small cups that were filled with frankincense and burned on top of the bread (see Leviticus 24:7 and Numbers 7:14).

*The covers,* or bowls, according to the best authorities, were the flagons such as were used for the rite of the drink offering, which appears to have regularly accompanied every meat offering (see Leviticus 23:18; Numbers 6:15; 28:14).

All these vessels were made of pure gold and speak of Christ in the various ways in which He presents to us, by the Spirit, the Bread of life. When the Lord Jesus promised the Comforter, He said: "He shall glorify Me: for He shall receive of Mine, and shall show it unto you" (John 16:14). So in each of these utensils we see the variegated glory of Christ to cause our souls to want to feed on Him the more.

The frankincense upon the bread speaks of His preciousness. No wonder Peter says: "Unto you . . . which believe He is precious" (1 Peter 2:7).

b. *The Measurements.* Thou shalt make a table of shittim wood, two cubits in length, one cubit in breadth, and one-and-a-half cubits in height (Exodus 25:23). The measurements imply limitation and restriction, but we can learn from this that the table was large enough for all who were worthy to come, which is the whole priesthood; and small enough to exclude all who were not worthy.

Before the institution of the Last Supper, you remember, Judas went out into the night. No traitor or unbeliever has a right to eat of Christ unless he comes with true penitence and faith. The warning concerning the Lord's table states: "Let a man examine himself, and so let him eat of that bread, and drink of that cup. . . . He that eateth and drinketh unworthily, eateth and drinketh damnation to himself, not discerning the Lord's body" (1 Corinthians 11:28-29).

It is interesting to observe here that while the sinful and unregenerate were excluded from the priesthood, whatever their bodily imperfections, the priests were included in the privilege of eating (see Leviticus 21:16-22). A priest had to be perfect in body to serve, but not necessarily perfect in body to eat.

Instructions were also given as to the making of the bread. We read that two tenth deals should be in one cake (Leviticus 24:5). Each of these loaves, therefore, represented the food of a man and his neighbor. The twelve loaves represented the twelve tribes, and there was a fresh supply every Sabbath (Leviticus 24:5-9). The priests ate the bread as God's representatives of the nation. All this is truly significant. Our Lord Jesus Christ is God's fresh and full supply for His people. It is only when we get away from the Father's home, as did the prodigal, that we have to cry: "How many hired servants of my father's have bread enough and to spare, and I perish with hunger!" (Luke 15:17)

c. *The Ministry.* The supreme ministry of the table of showbread, with its vessels, was to provide food and fellowship for God's priestly people.

1) *The Food.* "Thou shalt set upon the table showbread before Me alway" (Exodus 25:30). This was bread of a superlative quality. It was made of fine flour, the product of the earth and the necessity of man. The human body of Jesus Christ is seen here. His earthly life was like fine flour, perfect

in its whiteness and evenness. Pilate had to testify to this when he said, "I find no fault in this man" (Luke 23:4). Our Lord Jesus Christ in suffering was the fine flour kneaded and baked, so that He could become the Bread of life to us. "The bread that I will give is My flesh, which I will give for the life of the world" (John 6:51). This, then, is the food on which we can feed to our everlasting satisfaction.

The table also speaks of:

2) *Fellowship.* So we hear the Lord Jesus saying: "Behold, I stand at the door, and knock: if any man hear My voice, and open the door, I will come in to him, and will sup with him, and he with Me" (Revelation 3:20). Let us see to it that we do not abuse this wonderful fellowship. Paul warns us: "I would not that ye should have fellowship with devils. Ye cannot drink the cup of the Lord, and the cup of devils: ye cannot be partakers of the Lord's table, and of the table of devils. Do we provoke the Lord to jealousy? are we stronger than He?" (1 Corinthians 10:20-22) Let us never allow anything to spoil fellowship with Him at His table, both in the personal sense of our daily devotions, and in the corporate sense of sharing in Holy Communion.


## III. THE ALTAR OF INCENSE

### (Exodus 30:1-10,34-38; 37:25-28)

"Thou shalt make an altar to burn incense upon: of shittim wood shalt thou make it" (Exodus 30:1). The third article of furniture in the holy place was the altar of incense. Like the rest of the Tabernacle, it was constructed by a direct command. Let us note:

1. The Scriptural Specifications

The altar stood directly before the entrance to the

Tabernacle, though further within than either of the other two pieces of furniture. Its position was before the veil. It was only a small piece of furniture, standing two cubits high, one cubit broad, and one cubit long — just large enough to serve its purpose. It was made of acacia wood, overlaid with pure gold. It was surrounded by a golden crown, which kept the fire from falling to the ground. It had a horn on each of the four corners and was supplied with rings and staves for portability. Its purpose was for the burning of incense, compounded in equal proportions of stacte, and onycha, galbanum with frankincense.

2.  The Spiritual Significance

Consider first:

a. *The Materials.* The two main items for our examination are the altar and the incense.

1) *The Altar.* "And thou shalt make an altar . . . and . . . shalt overlay it with pure gold, the top thereof, and the sides thereof round about, and the horns thereof; and thou shalt make unto it a crown of gold round about. And two golden rings shalt thou make to it under the crown of it" (Exodus 30:1,3-4). Once again, the twofold nature of our Lord Jesus Christ is prefigured in the acacia wood and the pure gold. In the crown we see Him as the exalted One, seated at the right hand of the throne of God as our Intercessor. So it is written: "He is able also to save them to the uttermost that come unto God by Him, seeing that He ever liveth to make intercession for them" (Hebrews 7:25).

The horns, as we have already seen in the brazen altar, speak of power; but this time of power in prayer. Who is it that strengthens our petitions but our Lord Jesus Christ? So John says: "We have an advocate with the Father, Jesus Christ the righteous" (1 John 2:1).

The rings and staves, once again, speak of movement and mobility; and what a joy it is to know that we can offer prayer anywhere, at any time. Paul says: "I will therefore that men pray every where, lifting up holy hands, without wrath and doubting" (1 Timothy 2:8). Jesus reminded the woman of Samaria that worship and prayer would no longer be localized: "The hour cometh, when ye shall neither in this mountain, nor yet at Jerusalem, worship the Father. . . . They that worship Him must worship Him in spirit and in truth" (John 4:21,24).

So the altar of incense identifies us with our great Advocate, who waits to receive our expressions of adoration and intercession, and present them faultless to His Father in Heaven. It only remains to add that before the altar of incense could have any acceptance before God, it had to be sprinkled with the blood of the atonement. The solemn word was: "Aaron shall make an atonement upon the horns of it once in a year with the blood of the sin offering" (Exodus 30:10). So we see that our great High Priest advocates for us, and our approach in prayer is on the basis of grace.

2) *The Incense.* "And the LORD said unto Moses, Take unto thee sweet spices, stacte, and onycha, and galbanum; these sweet spices with pure frankincense: of each shall there be a like weight. . . . Whosoever shall make like unto that, to smell thereto, shall even be cut off from his people" (Exodus 30:34,38). The value of the altar lay in the incense. As we might expect, this incense typifies the merits of our great Saviour and Intercessor. It was made by the compounding of three spices of equal proportions, to which was added the same weight of frankincense. What these spices are no one can finally tell, but someone has suggested that in the stacte we see the merit of Christ's life; in the onycha, the merit of His death; in the galbanum, the merit of His resurrection; to which is added the frankincense of His ascension. No one can say which of them is most important: they are of equal value and all necessary.

You will have noticed in the reading that no one was allowed to compound anything like it, without being cut off from his people. Nadab and Abihu attempted to offer strange fire to God, and they were at once slain before the Lord. Likewise, to come to God in the virtue of our own merits is an unspeakable abomination. It is only as we name the Name of our Lord Jesus Christ and all His merits, fired by the flame of God's acceptance, that we can truly touch the throne. (It is suggested that the incense was put on the altar while the priest trimmed the lamps. Thus the incense of prayer and the lamp of testimony must always be viewed together.)

b. *The Measurements.* "A cubit shall be the length thereof, and a cubit the breadth thereof; foursquare shall it be . . . the horns thereof shall be of the same" (Exodus 30:2). It is interesting to note that it was two cubits high, which means that it was higher than any other of the articles of the holy place. Perhaps the suggestion in this height is that as our Intercessor God has raised Him from the dead and set Him "far above all" (Ephesians 1:21). He is now Head over all the Church.

The altar was foursquare, which speaks again of the availability of our Lord in prayer from any part of the earth. As to its position, it stood not only in the center of the holy place, but in a straight line with the brazen altar, the laver, the ark of the covenant, and the mercy seat. How instructive to note that this straight line represents the articles that speak of the divine provision for our approach unto God. Notice also that it stood immediately before the mercy seat, which is the throne of God. How near God comes to us in prayer — perhaps nearer than at any other time. In those days a veil separated the altar of incense from the ark of the covenant, but today there is not even a veil, for it has been rent from top to bottom.

c. *The Ministry.* As already anticipated in much of what has been said, the ministry of the altar of incense was that of adoration and intercession.

1) *Adoration.* The priests never came to offer incense without giving thanks to God. The writer to the Hebrews reminds us that we ought to do likewise. "By Him therefore let us offer the sacrifice of praise to God continually, that is, the fruit of our lips giving thanks to His name" (13:15).

2) *Intercession.* The Psalmist could say: "Let my prayer be set forth before Thee as incense; and the lifting up of my hands as the evening sacrifice" (141:2).

When Zacharias was burning incense in the Temple of the Lord, we read that the people were praying without (Luke 1:8-10). The fragrance from this sweet incense was continual. Ere the morning fragrance had died the evening burning commenced. So Christ ever lives to make intercession for us, and we through Him may offer our acts of adoration and intercession. What a blessed privilege is ours!

So we have seen something of the symbolism and spiritual significance of these three articles of furniture in the holy place. In the candlestick we learn the secret of illumination; in the table of showbread the source of satisfaction; and in the altar of incense we experience the strength of intercession. They are all inseparable to a life of worship and witness in the holy place. Let us see to it that we do not neglect our "so great salvation."

Chapter 8

# THE FURNITURE IN THE HOLY OF HOLIES

## *Scriptures for Study*

And they shall make an ark of shittim wood: two cubits and a half shall be the length thereof, and a cubit and a half the breadth thereof, and a cubit and a half the height thereof. And thou shalt overlay it with pure gold, within and without shalt thou overlay it, and shalt make upon it a crown of gold round about. And thou shalt cast four rings of gold for it, and put them in the four corners thereof; and two rings shall be in the one side of it, and two rings in the other side of it. And thou shalt make staves of shittim wood, and overlay them with gold. And thou shalt put the staves into the rings by the sides of the ark, that the ark may be borne with them. The staves shall be in the rings of the ark: they shall not be taken from it. And thou shalt put into the ark the testimony which I shall give thee.

And thou shalt make a mercy seat of pure gold: two cubits and a half shall be the length thereof, and a cubit and a half the breadth thereof. And thou shalt make two cherubims of gold, of beaten work shalt thou make them, in the two ends of the mercy seat. And make one cherub on the one end, and the other cherub on the other end: even of the mercy seat shall ye make the cherubims on the two ends thereof. And the cherubims shall stretch forth their wings on high, covering the mercy seat with their wings, and their faces shall look one to another; toward the mercy seat shall the faces of the cherubims be. And thou shalt put the mercy seat above upon the ark; and in the ark thou shalt put the testimony that I shall give thee. And there I will meet with thee, and I will commune with thee from above the mercy seat, from between the two cherubims which are upon the ark of the testimony, of all things which I will give thee in commandment unto the children of Israel (Exodus 25:10-22).

And Bezaleel made the ark of shittim wood: two cubits and a half was the length of it, and a cubit and a half the breadth of it, and a cubit and a half the height of it: And he overlaid it with pure gold within and without, and made a crown of gold to it round about. And he cast for it four rings of gold, to be set by the four corners of it; even two rings upon the one side of it, and two rings upon the other side of it. And he made staves of shittim wood, and overlaid them with gold. And he put the staves into the rings by the sides of the ark, to bear the ark.

And he made the mercy seat of pure gold: two cubits and a half was the length thereof, and one cubit and a half the breadth thereof. And he made two cherubims of gold, beaten out of one piece made he them, on the two ends of the mercy seat; One cherub on the end on this side, and another cherub on the other end on that side: out of the mercy seat made he the cherubims on the two ends thereof. And the cherubims spread out their wings on high, and covered with their wings over the mercy seat, with their faces one to another; even to the mercy seatward were the faces of the cherubims (Exodus 37:1-9; see also Exodus 16:11-31; 19; 20:1-17; Numbers 11:1-9; 16; 17; Psalm 78:24-25; Matthew 22:36-40; John 6:30-38; Revelation 2:7).

## THE FURNITURE IN THE HOLY OF HOLIES

Scriptures for Study: Exodus 25:10-22; 37:1-9; 16:11-31; 19; 20:1-17; Numbers 11:1-9; 16—17; Psalm 78:24-25; Matthew 22:36-40; John 6:30-38; Revelation 2:7

### I. THE ARK OF THE COVENANT

1.   The Scriptural Specifications

2.   The Spiritual Significance
     a. The Materials
        1) The Ark
        2) The Manna
        3) The Rod

The two pieces of furniture in the holiest of all were the ark of the covenant and the mercy seat. Although these two appeared as one article, they are, in fact, referred to quite distinctly. We shall follow our normal procedure in considering these separately, and then endeavor to show their vital link one to the other in the service they rendered in the Tabernacle and their meaning today for us.

## I. THE ARK OF THE COVENANT

### (Exodus 25:10-16; 27:1-9)

"And they shall make an ark of shittim wood: two cubits and a half shall be the length thereof, and a cubit and a half the breadth thereof, and a cubit and a half the height thereof. And thou shalt overlay it with pure gold, within and without shalt thou overlay it, and shalt make upon it a crown of gold round about" (Exodus 25:10-11).

In our study of the furniture of the Tabernacle, we have proceeded from the outer court, through the holy place, into the holy of holies. In other words, our approach has been the human one; but in the divine instructions to Moses we notice that God begins where we conclude. The very first articles to be constructed were the ark and the mercy seat. These were the most important of all the vessels of the Tabernacle, and the ones to which every other part of the building and its furniture had reference. The ark, with its mercy seat, was the throne of God. Here God focused His divine presence throughout all the years the Tabernacle was in existence, and until Solomon's Temple was built. No wonder the innermost place of the Tabernacle was called the holy of holies.

1. The Scriptural Specifications

The ark was a chest or box made of acacia wood, overlaid within and without with pure gold. Its length was two-and-a-half cubits, its breadth one-and-a-half cubits, and its height one-and-a-half cubits. Surrounding its top was a crown of gold, which held the precious mercy seat and cherubim. Two rings on each side at the base, with staves, made the ark portable. Inside the ark were four items of supreme significance: the two tables of the law (Exodus 25:16), the book of the covenant (Exodus 24:7), the pot with an omer of manna (Exodus 16:33; Hebrews 9:4), and Aaron's rod that budded (Numbers 17:10; Hebrews 9:4).

2. The Spiritual Significance

As in our previous studies, we shall consider the spiritual significance of each of the articles in the holiest of all, in terms of the materials, the measurements, and the ministry.

a. *The Materials.* The ark and its contents, as we should expect, speak pre-eminently of our Lord Jesus Christ. Here, as perhaps in no other articles of furniture, is centered the meaning of His Person and work. Let us look at the items in order of their mention.

1) *The Ark.* "And they shall make an ark of shittim wood. . . . And thou shalt overlay it with pure gold, within and without . . . and shalt make upon it a crown of gold round about" (Exodus 25:10,11). Here once more we are brought face to face with our Lord in His twofold nature. In the acacia wood we see His perfect humanity, while in the pure gold His perfect divinity. Notice that the overlay of gold was "within and without," speaking of the reality of that divine nature. There are those who would tell us that the Lord Jesus became divine only when the Spirit of God came upon Him as a dove at His baptism; but that is heresy. John the Apostle warns us of the false prophets who are gone into the world. He says: "Hereby know ye the Spirit of God: Every spirit that confesseth that Jesus Christ is come in the flesh is of God" (1 John 4:2). In other words, the Spirit of truth is He who witnesses not only to the pre-existence of Christ, but to the manifestation of God of very God in the flesh: pure gold within and without.

We notice also that the ark was surrounded by a *crown* of solid gold. Man crowned Him with thorns, but God has crowned Him with glory and honor (Hebrews 2:9), and set Him at His own right hand.

The four *rings* of gold and the two *staves* speak of His constancy and availability to all the people of God. There is no beginning nor end to a ring, which teaches us that our Lord Jesus is "the same yesterday, and to day, and for ever" (Hebrews 13:8). The staves remind us of His word, when He says: "I will never leave thee, nor forsake thee" (Hebrews 13:5).

So the ark points to our ascended Lord as Son of God and Son of Man, crowned with glory, ever living, and ever present to all who call upon Him.

2) *The Manna.* The writer to the Hebrews reminds us that within the ark of the covenant was "the golden pot that

had manna" (9:4). Moses was commanded to "take a pot, and put an omer full of manna therein, and lay it up before the LORD, to be kept for your generations" (Exodus 16:33-34). This manna, which in the Hebrew means, "What is it?" in the Chaldean, "It is a portion," and in the English, "bread," was God's miraculous and bountiful provision for His ancient people throughout their journeying in the wilderness.

If Exodus 16:11-31 and Numbers 11:1-9 are studied carefully, it will be noted in every detail that the manna speaks of Christ as the Bread of life. Indeed, the Lord Jesus likened the manna to His own Person in that instructive discourse in John 6:31-38.

From the description given us of the manna in the passage already referred to, we learn that it was "small" (Exodus 16:14), speaking of the *humility* of Christ — He "made Himself of no reputation" (Philippians 2:7); "round" (Exodus 16:14), speaking of the *perfection* of Christ — "(the only begotten of the Father,) full of grace and truth" (John 1:14); "white" (Exodus 16:31), speaking of the *holiness* of Christ — "holy, harmless, undefiled, separate from sinners" (Hebrews 7:26); "as the hoar frost" (Exodus 16:14), speaking of the *freshness* of Christ. He could say: "The words that I speak unto you, they are spirit, and they are life" (John 6:63); "like coriander seed" (Exodus 16:31), speaking of the *fragrance* of Christ — "thy name is as ointment poured forth" (Song of Solomon 1:3); "as the taste of fresh oil" (Numbers 11:8), speaking of the *authority* of Christ as the Anointed One — "He whom God hath sent speaketh the words of God: for God giveth not the Spirit by measure unto Him" (John 3:34); "like wafers made with honey" (Exodus 16:31), speaking of the *sweetness* of Christ — "I sat down under his shadow with great delight, and his fruit was sweet to my taste" (Song of Solomon 2:3); "as the colour of bdellium" (Numbers 11:7), speaking of the *preciousness* of Christ (bdellium is thought to be the beryl crystal) — "Unto you . . . which believe He is precious" (1 Peter 2:7). What a comprehensive picture this is of the Lord Jesus!

We notice further that this manna was:

*A Sufficient Provision.* "He that gathered little had no lack; they gathered every man according to his eating" (Exodus 16:18). So God provided for His people throughout the forty years. This Bread from Heaven never failed.

*A Satisfying Provision.* "The taste of it was like wafers made with honey" (Exodus 16:31). Jewish authorities tell us that "it tasted to every man as he pleased." In other words, it suited every palate, young and old, weak and strong; a truly remarkable fact when one considers that there were some two-and-a-half million people to satisfy.

*A Sustaining Provision.* "And the children of Israel did eat manna forty years, until they came to a land inhabited: they did eat manna, until they came unto the borders of the land of Canaan" (Exodus 16:35). The nutrition in this bread from Heaven must have contained all the required vitamins, for it maintained the strength of this pilgrim nation right throughout the forty years of their wilderness wandering.

So in the Lord Jesus we, too, find our sufficiency, satisfaction, and sustenance. He could say: "I am the living bread which came down from heaven: if any man eat of this bread, he shall live for ever: and the bread that I will give is My flesh, which I will give for the life of the world" (John 6:51).

3) *The Rod.* Within the ark was a pot that had manna, and Aaron's rod that budded (Hebrews 9:4). This rod was the emblem of God's chosen priesthood. The circumstances in which it budded are recorded for us in Numbers 16 and 17. There had been a rebellion against the priesthood of Moses and Aaron; and God had to judge the rebels and then

vindicate the authority and ministry of His chosen servants. So a rod (which was the tribal staff, suitably named), was taken from each of the twelve tribes and laid before Jehovah in the tent of meeting. Among these was Aaron's rod. Here then were twelve sticks, dead, separated from mother earth, the source of all vegetable life. They were allowed to lie overnight, and in the morning Moses went to examine them, and we read that "the rod of Aaron for the house of Levi was budded, and brought forth buds, and bloomed blossoms, and yielded almonds" (Numbers 17:8).

What rich teaching is enshrined in this rod that budded, blossomed, and brought forth almonds! In the rod we have a picture of the Saviour's incarnation. He was "as a root out of a dry ground" (Isaiah 53:2). Later on we read that "He was cut off out of the land of the living" (Isaiah 53:8). The buds speak of His resurrection. Having died for our sins, the third day He rose again, according to the Scriptures (1 Corinthians 15:4). In the truest sense, Christ is the only One who ever rose from the dead. Both in the Old and New Testaments, men and women and children were resuscitated to a fresh lease of life, but subsequently they died again. F. B. Meyer pointedly remarks that in each case there was one cradle, but two coffins! As far as our Lord Jesus Christ is concerned, however, "in that He died, He died unto sin once: but in that He liveth, He liveth unto God" (Romans 6:10). "Christ being raised from the dead dieth no more; death hath no more dominion over Him" (Romans 6:9).

In the blossoms we see His exaltation, for the flower is ever the glory of the tree. After His resurrection we read that He was "received up into glory" (1 Timothy 3:16).

The almonds typify His reproduction. The manifestation of life is beauty; and the purpose of beauty, all through God's fair creation, is the reproduction of life for the maintenance of succeeding generations. So our Lord Jesus

Christ from Heaven is reproducing His life in every sinner who repents and believes. Isaiah tells us that, having made His soul an offering for sin, "He shall see His seed, He shall prolong His days" (53:10). So the risen Christ has a seed, and one day He will present the precious fruit that He has produced, saying, "Behold I and the children which God hath given Me" (Hebrews 2:13). The Psalmist also tells us that "a seed shall serve Him; it shall be accounted to the Lord for a generation" (22:30).

4) *The Two Tables of the Law.* In the ark was "the golden pot that had manna, and Aaron's rod that budded, and the tables of the covenant" (Hebrews 9:4). The instruction to Moses was: "And thou shalt put into the ark the testimony which I shall give thee" (Exodus 25:16). The testimony was the moral law, written on two tables of stone, consisting of the Ten Commandments which are detailed for us in Exodus 20:1-17. The law, which men and women could not keep, was deposited within the ark of the covenant and beneath the mercy seat — a type of the only One who kept the whole law.

In the words of prophecy, we hear our Lord Jesus saying: "Lo, I come: in the volume of the book it was written of Me, I delight to do Thy will, O My God: yea, Thy law is within My heart" (Psalm 40:7-8). When He appeared in the flesh, He could say: "Think not that I am come to destroy the law, or the prophets: I am not come to destroy, but to fulfil" (Matthew 5:17). The Apostle Paul reminds us that "Christ is the end of the law for righteousness to every one that believeth" (Romans 10:4).

5) *The Book of the Covenant.* In Exodus 24:7 we read that Moses "took the book of the covenant, and read in the audience of the people: and they said, All that the LORD hath said will we do, and be obedient." Later in Deuteronomy 31:25-26, "Moses commanded the Levites,

which bare the ark of the covenant of the LORD, saying, Take this book of the law, and put it in the side of the ark of the covenant of the LORD your God, that it may be there for a witness against thee." It has been suggested that the contents of the book of the covenant consisted of certain sections of Exodus, e.g., 20, 22, 23, 33, such as we have in our Old Testament today. It included such laws as those appertaining to murder, property, divorce, servants, injuries, and so on.

If the two tables of the testimony represented the moral law, the book of the covenant stands for the civil law. As in the moral law, so in the civil law our Lord Jesus is the final embodiment of God's thought. When on earth He declared: "Ye have heard that it hath been said, An eye for an eye, and a tooth for a tooth: But I say unto you, That ye resist not evil; but whosoever shall smite thee on thy right cheek, turn to him the other also" (Matthew 5:38-39). Just as the civil law was contained in the ark of the covenant, so God's ideal for men and women was outworked in the life of the Lord Jesus in human history.

b. *The Measurements.* "And they shall make an ark of shittim wood: two cubits and a half shall be the length thereof, and a cubit and a half the breadth thereof, and a cubit and a half the height thereof" (Exodus 25:10). It is agreed by most scholars that there is considerable difficulty in assigning a reason for each of the measurements of the ark. My own conviction is that the Holy Spirit does not intend that we should attempt to press into these measurements artificial meaning. We must remember that the holiest of all speaks of Heaven itself, and that the ark and the mercy seat speak of the Lord Jesus crowned and enthroned "Far above all principality, and power, and might, and dominion, and every name that is named, not only in this world, but also in that which is to come" (Ephesians 1:21). In view of this, what finite mind can possibly understand or interpret the comprehensiveness of our glorified Lord? When we contemplate the ark of the covenant, we must cry with the Apostle Paul: "O the depth of the riches both of the wisdom and knowledge of God! how unsearchable are His judgments, and His ways past finding out!" (Romans 11:33)

Under this heading of "measurements" we might observe, in passing, that in God's thought the ark was central to everything else. The first word from Heaven to Moses was: "Let them make Me a sanctuary; that I may dwell among them.... And they shall make an ark of shittim wood" (Exodus 25:8-10).

We build a house, and then think of the furniture afterwards; but not so with God. He would teach us that the ark speaks of His beloved Son, and that He is "before all things, and by Him all things consist" (Colossians 1:17).

c. *The Ministry.* Gathering up the lessons we have learned from the foregoing rich symbolism, we would say that in the ark we see Christ our All in all. The ark includes and sums up everything else in the Tabernacle and its furniture. So with the Apostle we can say: "Christ . . . is made unto us wisdom, and righteousness, and sanctification, and redemption" (1 Corinthians 1:30). As our "wisdom," He is our book of the covenant; as our "righteousness," He is the tables of testimony; as our "sanctification," He is the pot of manna; and as our "redemption," He is the rod that budded, for the final intention of our God in redemption is to produce eternal fruit unto His Name.

## II. THE MERCY SEAT

### (Exodus 25:17-22)

"And thou shalt make a mercy seat of pure gold: two cubits and a half shall be the length thereof, and a cubit and a half the breadth thereof. And thou shalt make two cherubims of gold, of beaten work shalt thou make them, in the two ends of the mercy seat. . . . And there I will meet with thee, and I will commune with thee from above the mercy seat" (Exodus 25:17,18,22). Here we come to the throne of the Tabernacle, where God manifested Himself in Shekinah glory, so we must tread reverently and softly, as we give ourselves to the examination of this exalted subject.

1. The Scriptural Specifications

The mercy seat was a slab of solid gold, two and a half by one and a half cubits, which fitted exactly inside the crown of the ark of the covenant. The cherubim were placed at the two ends of the mercy seat, not standing separately upon it, but of one beaten piece with the mercy seat. Their wings were raised to cover the mercy seat, and the faces were bent downwards, gazing at the mercy seat.

2. The Spiritual Significance

As the central seat of God's saving grace and presence, the mercy seat must invite our careful attention as we examine:

a. *The Materials.* "Thou shalt make a mercy seat of pure gold. . . . And thou shalt make two cherubims of gold, of beaten work shalt thou make them" (Exodus 25:17-18).

1) *The Mercy Seat.* This, as we have noted, was made of pure gold. No wood was used in its manufacture. This means that what is in view here is not so much the divinity of our Lord, as related to His humanity, but rather His divinity in relation to righteousness. Without divine righteousness being

satisfied by the shedding and application of blood, there could be no outflowing of grace to guilty men.

What does the mercy seat mean, and what does it stand for? We learn from both Old and New Testaments that it was the place of propitiation. Upon the mercy seat was the blood of propitiation, sprinkled every year on the Day of Atonement. No one knew this better than the Apostle Paul, who could speak of Christ as our Propitiation, or Mercy Seat. Consider these remarkable words of Romans 3:25: "Whom God hath set forth to be a propitiation through faith in His blood, to declare His righteousness for the remission of sins that are past, through the forbearance of God." John also has the same thought in view when he says: "Herein is love, not that we loved God, but that He loved us, and sent His Son to be the propitiation for our sins" (1 John 4:10). Because of the blood-sprinkled Mercy Seat, we can know reconciliation, forgiveness, justification, and peace.

2) *The Cherubim.* These, with the mercy seat, were of one beaten piece of pure gold. As we have seen already in these studies, the cherubim speak of divine justice. We meet them first in the very early chapters of the Bible, placed at the east of the Garden of Eden with "a flaming sword which turned every way, to keep the way of the tree of life" (Genesis 3:24). It is true that the progressive revelation gives us more light on them, as we see them appearing again in such books as the prophecy of Ezekiel, and later the Revelation, but essentially they are messengers of judgment. Here on the mercy seat they stand poised to strike, were it not for the blood-sprinkled mercy seat.

When God passed through Egypt in judgment, He first of all warned His own people to shelter 'neath the blood-sprinkled doorposts and lintels of their homes. The divine dictum was: "When I see the blood, I will pass over you" (Exodus 12:13). Similarly, here again, judgment holds back its sword because the blood has been shed and sprinkled. The sweet singer of Israel is right when he says: "Justice and judgment are the habitation of Thy throne: mercy and truth shall go before Thy face" (Psalm 89:14). Again: "Mercy and truth are met together; righteousness and peace have kissed each other" (Psalm 85:10).

b. *The Measurements.* The measurements of the mercy seat are as mysterious as those of the ark, telling us again that God's wisdom and love are infinite, and therefore past the comprehension of our finite minds. It is interesting and instructive to observe, however, that while the mercy seat was detachable, it was fitted so perfectly that it could not slip off the ark without cause. It was held fast by the crown that surrounded the ark.

How wonderful to know that God's abundant mercy to us is held fast by the crowning glory of His determination to save man. Jesus would never have been crowned with glory, had He not fulfilled God's perfect plan of redemption. So we can rest in the knowledge that the mercy seat will never become a throne of judgment until the elect are complete.

c. *The Ministry* of the mercy seat is beautifully summed up for us in the words of the Hebrew writer, when he invites us to "come boldly unto the throne of grace, that we may obtain mercy, and find grace to help in time of need" (Hebrews 4:16). What would have been a throne of judgment is for us a throne of grace, because Jesus, as the merciful and faithful High Priest, has made "reconciliation for the sins of the people" (Hebrews 2:17). So we praise God for the mercy seat, where we can find grace to help "in the nick of time."

Thus we have seen in the ark of the covenant and in the mercy seat a glorious picture of our exalted Lord, who comes out to us in mercy because of the work He accomplished at Calvary's cross. In the ark of the covenant we have presented a sufficient Saviour, while in the mercy seat we have portrayed to us an efficient Saviour. How well we can sing with the hymnwriter:

> All that I "need" is in Jesus;
>   He satisfies, joy He supplies;
> Life would be worthless without Him,
>   All things in Jesus I find.
>
> Harry Dixon Loes

# Chapter 9

## THE PRIESTHOOD

### *Scriptures for Study*

For every high priest taken from among men is ordained for men in things pertaining to God, that he may offer both gifts and sacrifices for sins: Who can have compassion on the ignorant, and on them that are out of the way; for that he himself also is compassed with infirmity. And by reason hereof he ought, as for the people, so also for himself, to offer for sins. And no man taketh this honour unto himself, but he that is called of God, as was Aaron.

So also Christ glorified not Himself to be made an high priest; but He that said unto Him, Thou art My Son, to day have I begotten Thee. As He saith also in another place, Thou art a priest for ever after the order of Melchisedec. Who in the days of His flesh, when He had offered up prayers and supplications with strong crying and tears unto Him that was able to save Him from death, and was heard in that He feared; Though He were a Son, yet learned He obedience by the things which He suffered; And being made perfect, He became the author of eternal salvation unto all them that obey Him; Called of God an high priest after the order of Melchisedec (Hebrews 5:1-10; see also Exodus 28—29; Leviticus 8).

THE PRIESTHOOD

Scriptures for Study: Hebrews 5:1-10; Exodus 28–29; Leviticus 8

### I.  AARON AND HIS GOD

1. Priestly Appointment
    a.  His Purification
    b.  His Sanctification

2. Priestly Apparel
    a.  The Coat
    b.  The Robe
    c.  The Ephod
        1) The Shoulder Stones
        2) The Breastplate
        3) The Urim and Thummim
        4) The Curious Girdle
    d.  The Miter

3. Priestly Activity
    a.  The Charge of the Sacrifices
    b.  The Charge of the Service

### II.  AARON AND HIS SONS

1. Called

2. Cleansed
    a.  A Judicial Cleansing
    b.  A Moral Cleansing

3. Clothed
    a.  Coats — salvation
    b.  Girdles — service

  c. The Bonnets — subjection
  d. The Breeches — self-effacement
4. Consecrated
  a. Personal Dedication
  b. Moral Separation
    1) Separation from Sin
    2) Separation unto Service
  c. Spiritual Realization

## III. AARON AND THE LEVITES

1. Purified

2. Mobilized

3. Utilized

Hitherto we have studied the Tabernacle in relation to its purpose, erection, structure, coverings, and furniture. The main emphasis of truth has been that of God coming out to man. Now we turn from the Tabernacle and its furniture to the priesthood, when our chief consideration will be that of man coming into the presence of God.

In general terms, the priesthood consisted of Aaron, his sons, and his tribe. So if we would understand the constitution and function of the priesthood, we must keep this threefold distinction in mind. As we proceed with our study, we shall observe that when Aaron is considered alone, he represents the priestly ministry of the Christ of God. Aaron with his sons typifies the priestly ministry of the Church of God, while Aaron and his tribe illustrate the priestly ministry of the children of God, with emphasis on the individual believer, rather than the corporate action of the Church.

Let us then first consider:

## I. AARON AND HIS GOD

God's words to Moses were: "Take thou unto thee Aaron thy brother . . . from among the children of Israel, that he may minister unto Me in the priest's office. . . . And thou shalt make holy garments for Aaron thy brother for glory and for beauty" (Exodus 28:1-2). Here we have Aaron's:

1. Priestly Appointment

The writer to the Hebrews reminds us that "every high priest taken from among men is ordained for men in things pertaining to God, that he may offer both gifts and sacrifices for sins. . . . And no man taketh this honour unto himself, but he that is called of God, as was Aaron" (Hebrews 5:1,4). This appointment, or ordination, of Aaron involved two initial and important acts:

a. *His Purification.* "And Aaron . . . thou shalt bring unto the door of the tabernacle of the congregation, and shalt wash . . . with water" (Exodus 29:4). Having been taken from among the children of Israel, it now had to be demonstrated publicly that he was morally suitable and acceptable to serve as God's high priest.

How this reminds us of the appointment of our Lord Jesus Christ as the *Great* High Priest. We read: "Verily He took not on Him the nature of angels; but He took on Him the seed of Abraham. Wherefore in all things it behoved Him to be made like unto His brethren, that He might be a merciful and faithful high priest in things pertaining to God, to make reconciliation for the sins of the people" (Hebrews 2:16-17).

Having been taken from among His brethren, He was washed publicly to demonstrate His suitability and acceptability as High Priest before God. That event took place at His baptism in Jordan. Though He had no sins to repent of, and no defilement which required washing away, yet He submitted Himself to the act of purification. Addressing John the Baptist, who attempted to forbid His being baptized, Jesus said: "Suffer it to be so now: for thus it becometh us to fulfil all righteousness. Then he suffered Him" (Matthew 3:15). His moral qualification for being God's High Priest was confirmed when Heaven opened and the Voice declared: "This is My beloved Son, in whom I am well pleased" (Matthew 3:17).

b. *His Sanctification.* "Then shalt thou take the anointing oil, and pour it upon his head, and anoint him" (Exodus 29:7). It is important to note that Aaron was anointed here *alone,* typifying our Lord Jesus Christ as high priest. Then later he was anointed with his sons, representing the priesthood of all believers.

Following the act of purification in Jordan, there was the act of sanctification of our Great High Priest. Jesus spoke of this sanctification when He referred to Himself as the One "whom the Father hath sanctified, and sent into the world" (John 10:36). At the end of His life He could say in His high priestly prayer: "And for their sakes I sanctify Myself, that they also might be sanctified through the truth" (John 17:19). Matthew tells us that: "Jesus, when He was baptized, went up straightway out of the water: and, lo, the heavens were opened unto Him, and he saw the Spirit of God descending like a dove, and lighting upon Him" (Matthew 3:16).

Here was the setting apart for His life's ministry. Referring to this moment, and quoting from the Old Testament, the Hebrew writer says: "Thou hast loved righteousness, and hated iniquity; therefore God, even Thy God, hath anointed Thee with the oil of gladness above Thy fellows" (Hebrews 1:9).

Isaiah prophesies the same event when he puts these words into the mouth of the Lord Jesus: "The Spirit of the

Lord GOD is upon Me; because the LORD hath anointed Me to preach good tidings unto the meek; He hath sent Me to bind up the brokenhearted, to proclaim liberty to the captives, and the opening of the prison to them that are bound" (Isaiah 61:1). Needless to say, this anointing included not only His ministry as Priest, but as Prophet and King. So we may say with another: "Consider the Apostle and High Priest of our profession, Christ Jesus; Who was faithful to Him that appointed Him" (Hebrews 3:1-2).

Following Aaron's priestly appointment, we have his:

2. Priestly Apparel

"Thou shalt make holy garments for Aaron . . . for glory and for beauty" (Exodus 28:2). The glory and beauty of these garments were designed not so much to draw attention to Aaron himself as to the sacredness and holiness of his office. Each part of his attire speaks eloquently of the glories, virtues, and excellencies of our Great High Priest, the Lord Jesus Christ.

Altogether there were seven main pieces of apparel, speaking of His perfection as high priest. Let us consider Aaron's attire in the order in which he was dressed:

a. *The Coat.* "And thou shalt take the garments, and put upon Aaron the coat" (Exodus 29:5). This speaks of the *humanity* of Christ our Great High Priest. It was the innermost garment, and the divine instructions concerning it were as follows: "Thou shalt embroider the coat of fine linen . . . and thou shalt make the girdle of needlework" (Exodus 28:39). Fine twined linen speaks of His perfect human life. He was "holy, harmless, undefiled, separate from sinners" (Hebrews 7:26).

Connected with the coat was the *girdle* of fine twined linen. This speaks of the manward side of the service of our Lord Jesus Christ. He could say to His disciples: "The Son of man came not to be ministered unto, but to minister, and to give His life a ransom for many" (Matthew 20:28). How we see this matchlessly demonstrated in His life on earth as He "went about doing good" (Acts 10:38). Then at the close of His ministry we see Him girding Himself with a towel to wash the disciples' feet (John 13:4-5), and from that point moving right on to the cross to make atonement for sin.

It is significant that on the great Day of Atonement the high priest did not wear his garments of glory and beauty, but this coat of fine linen. Similarly, our Lord Jesus went to Calvary, not in His claims to universal dominion, nor in His kingship over the Jews, but in the perfection of His human life. Truly, "we have not an high priest which cannot be touched with the feeling of our infirmities; but was in all points tempted like as we are, yet without sin" (Hebrews 4:15).

b. *The Robe.* "And thou shalt take the garments, and put upon Aaron . . . the robe of the ephod" (Exodus 29:5). This speaks of the *divinity* of Christ as our Great High Priest. It was the second layer of attire, and the divine instructions concerning it were as follows: "Thou shalt make the robe of the ephod all of blue. And there shall be an hole in the top of it, in the midst thereof: it shall have a binding of woven work round about the hole of it . . . that it be not rent. And beneath upon the hem of it thou shalt make pomegranates of blue, and of purple, and of scarlet, round about the hem thereof; and bells of gold between them round about" (Exodus 28:31-33).

Blue, as we have seen before, is the heavenly color, and typifies the divine character of our Lord. Though "made like unto His brethren," our Saviour was nevertheless God of very God. The message of the angels at the birth of Jesus was: "Fear not: for, behold, I bring you good tidings of great joy. . . . For unto you is born . . . a Saviour, which is Christ the Lord" (Luke 2:10-11). Then as "holy brethren, partakers of the heavenly calling," we are exhorted to "consider the Apostle and High Priest of our profession, Christ Jesus" (Hebrews 3:1).

You will have observed that the robe was without seam, curiously wrought so as to prevent its being torn (Exodus 28:32). What attacks are made on the deity and divinity of our Lord Jesus Christ; and yet it cannot be denied that "without controversy ... God was manifest in the flesh" (1 Timothy 3:16).

Attached to the skirt of this robe were *golden bells* and *pomegranates.* The bells speak of testimony, while the pomegranates typify fruitfulness. The number of bells was equal to the number of pomegranates. This is of challenging significance. If fruitfulness speaks of our walk, and testimony of our talk, it shows how balanced was the life of our Lord Jesus: walk equaled talk, and talk equaled walk. How often our experience proves to be just the opposite!

c. *The Ephod.* "And thou shalt take the garments, and put upon Aaron ... the ephod, and the breastplate, and gird him with the curious girdle of the ephod" (Exodus 29:5). This speaks of the *ability* of Christ our Great High Priest. It was the outer garment, and instructions concerning it were detailed and minute: "They shall make the ephod of gold, of blue, and of purple, of scarlet, and fine twined linen, with cunning work ... and the curious girdle of the ephod, which is upon it, shall be of the same ... and thou shalt take two onyx stones, and grave on them the names of the children of Israel ... and thou shalt put the two stones upon the shoulders of the ephod ... and thou shalt make the breastplate of judgment ... and thou shalt set it in settings of stones ... and the stones shall be with the names of the children of Israel ... and thou shalt put in the breastplate of judgment the Urim and the Thummim" (Exodus 28:6-30). The materials employed to make the ephod sum up all the essential characteristics of the Person of our Lord Jesus Christ. There was gold, blue, purple, scarlet, and linen, all wrought with cunning work.

Attached to the ephod were the following:

1) *The Shoulder Stones* (Exodus 28:7-12). These were onyx stones upon which were graven the names of the children of Israel, typifying Christ's ability, as High Priest, to *keep* His own. The shoulders are the place of security and strength. When as Shepherd the Lord Jesus is pictured as finding the lost sheep, we read that "He layeth it on His shoulders, rejoicing" (Luke 15:5). How wonderful to know that, like the children of Israel, we, as His own, have a place on His shoulders of strength. No wonder Peter tells us that we are "kept by the power of God through faith unto salvation ready to be revealed in the last time" (1 Peter 1:5).

2) *The Breastplate.* This was a nine-inch, foursquare piece of linen cloth which was attached securely to the ephod, and contained twelve stones with the names of the children of Israel (Exodus 28:15-29). This breastplate typifies the ability of our High Priest to *love* His own. The breast is the place of affection, and our High Priest not only carries us on His shoulders, but on His heart. Paul reminds us in that glorious outburst of Christian certainty in Romans 8 that nothing "shall be able to separate us from the love of God, which is in Christ Jesus our Lord" (verse 39).

Each stone was a different color, equally precious and beautifully engraved, illustrating the Saviour's personal interest in each one of His people. Our Lord plainly said: "My sheep hear My voice, and I know them, and they follow Me: And I give unto them eternal life; and they shall never perish, neither shall any man pluck them out of My hand" (John 10:27-28).

3) *The Urim and Thummim* (Exodus 28:30). The names Urim and Thummim are Hebrew words denoting light and

perfection, or illumination and truth. It appears that these were two stones, possibly black and white, which were carried in the pouch of the breastplate. What they were and how they worked is not disclosed to us. It would seem that they were used for discerning the will of God in all matters of faith and practice. Some scholars have suggested that they either brightened or grew dim, according to God's "Yes" or "No" (see Numbers 27:21 and 1 Samuel 28:6). They typify the ability of Christ, as High Priest, to *guide* His own. Through the Holy Scriptures and the Holy Spirit, our Lord is ever guiding His people into the ways of truth and righteousness. Jesus said: "He that followeth Me shall not walk in darkness, but shall have the light of life" (John 8:12).

4) *The Curious Girdle* (Exodus 28:4,8). We have already seen that there was a plain girdle, speaking of Christ's service as man; but this girdle gathers up into itself all the characteristics of Christ as Son of Man and Son of God. It was made of the same material as the ephod; therefore it typifies the ability of Christ, as High Priest, to *serve* His own. As our High Priest at the right hand of the majesty on high, Christ is able to "succour them that are tempted" (Hebrews 2:18). Again: "This man, because He continueth ever, hath an unchangeable priesthood. Wherefore He is able also to save them to the uttermost that come unto God by Him, seeing He ever liveth to make intercession for them" (Hebrews 7:24-25).

One day this glorified Lord will return to serve His own in rewarding grace. Jesus said: "Blessed are those servants, whom the lord when He cometh shall find watching: verily I say unto you, that He shall gird Himself, and make them to sit down to meat, and will come forth and serve them" (Luke 12:37).

So in the ephod and its attachment we see the ability of Christ, as our High Priest, to keep us, love us, guide us, and serve us.

d. *The Miter.* "And thou shalt take the garments, and put upon Aaron . . . the miter . . . and put the holy crown upon the miter" (Exodus 29:5,6). This speaks of the *authority* of Christ as our Great High Priest. The miter was a turban of fine twisted linen, to which was attached a plate of pure gold, bearing the words "HOLINESS TO THE LORD" (Exodus 28:36).

The nature of all true authority consists of a subjection unto God and a perfection before God. In both these respects our Lord Jesus stands out as supreme. In His walk, words, and works He always claimed that He acted in subjection to His Father's authority. He could say: "I can of Mine own self do nothing: as I hear, I judge: and My judgment is just; because I seek not Mine own will, but the will of the Father which hath sent Me" (John 5:30). In this He acknowledged the headship of His God. Paul reminds us that "the head of Christ is God" (1 Corinthians 11:3). So as a Son He "learned . . . obedience by the things which He suffered" (Hebrews 5:8).

Then together with His subjection unto God there was His *perfection* before God. Twice over His Father could declare: "This is My beloved Son, in whom I am well pleased" (Matthew 3:17; 17:5). The Apostle Paul catches up these two thoughts of subjection and perfection when he declares the credentials of Jesus Christ as the Son of God in Romans 1:3-4: "Jesus Christ . . . declared to be the Son of God with power, according to the spirit of holiness, by the resurrection from the dead." His authority was based upon His life of subjection, in dependence upon the Spirit, and His walk of holiness, which guaranteed His resurrection from the dead.

What a great High Priest is ours! We have noted His humanity, divinity, ability, and authority. He is human and divine, able and all-powerful. How this should comfort our hearts!

So we have learned of Aaron's priestly appointment and apparel. Now consider his:

3. Priestly Activity

The work of Aaron the high priest can be summed up in seven words: to "keep the charge of the LORD" (Leviticus 8:35). In terms of the Tabernacle, this meant:

a. *The Charge of the Sacrifices.* "For every high priest taken from among men is ordained for men in things pertaining to God, that he may offer both gifts and sacrifices for sins" (Hebrews 5:1). Aaron's work, as high priest of Israel, was to sprinkle the blood upon and before the mercy seat on the great Day of Atonement, and thus make reconciliation for the sins of the people. In this great act of sacrifice is included all other gifts and sacrifices which he himself offered or supervised in the course of his daily ministry.

So with Aaron's Antitype, as One made like unto His brethren, He became "a merciful and faithful high priest in things pertaining to God, to make reconciliation for the sins of the people" (Hebrews 2:17). Unlike Aaron's sacrifices, our Great High Priest has offered one sacrifice for sins forever, and is seated at the right hand of God (Hebrews 10:11-12). There He acts as our Advocate with the Father (1 John 2:1), ministering forgiveness and cleansing, by virtue of His precious blood shed once and for all (1 John 1:7,9).

b. *The Charge of the Service.* God said: "I will sanctify . . . both Aaron and his sons, to minister to Me in the priest's office" (Exodus 29:44). Such service included trimming the lamps, burning the incense, arranging and dispensing the showbread, and appointing to his sons and the divisions of the tribe of Levi their respective service.

In a similar way, our Lord, as the Great High Priest, walks in the midst of the golden candlesticks (see Revelation 1), ministers at the golden altar (Revelation 8:3-4), feeds us with the living bread (John 6:51), and directs the ministry of the Church (Ephesians 4:8-16) so that "unto every one of us is given grace according to the measure of the gift of Christ" (Ephesians 4:7). Praise God for our Great High Priest!

## II. AARON AND HIS SONS

The Holy Spirit having focused our attention first of all on Aaron alone, now proceeds to link him with his sons, illustrating the priesthood of all believers within the sphere of the Church. What is now said of Aaron does not strictly apply to Christ. So we learn that Aaron and his sons were:

1. Called

"Take thou unto thee Aaron thy brother, and his sons with him, from among the children of Israel, that he may minister unto Me in the priest's office, even Aaron, Nadab and Abihu, Eleazar and Ithamar, Aaron's sons" (Exodus 28:1).

Likewise, through faith in our Lord Jesus Christ, we have been called to a "holy priesthood, to offer up spiritual sacrifices, acceptable to God by Jesus Christ" (1 Peter 2:5). Here is an essential truth in our evangelical faith, that without distinction all believers are priests unto God. The religious idea that one must, of necessity, have some man or order of men to act as mediators between God and men is a pernicious heresy and therefore utterly alien to the Word of God. As priests, in subjection to our Great High Priest, we have immediate access into the holy of holies: "There is one God, and one mediator between God and men, the man Christ Jesus" (1 Timothy 2:5).

2. Cleansed

"And Aaron and his sons thou shalt bring unto the door of the tabernacle of the congregation, and shalt wash them with water. . . . And thou shalt cause a bullock to be brought before the tabernacle of the congregation: and Aaron and his sons shall put their hands upon the head of the bullock" (Exodus 29:4,10). These verses teach us that there is a twofold cleansing which fits us as priests to come into the presence of God. There is, first of all:

a. *A Judicial Cleansing.* "And thou shalt kill the bullock before the LORD" (Exodus 29:11). The bullock was the sin offering which had to be slain and offered in a prescribed manner, in order to atone for Aaron and his sons. Only on the basis of shed and sprinkled blood could they qualify to worship and witness in the presence of God.

Similarly in our case, only the blood of the Lamb of God fits us for our priestly ministry. So John the divine exclaims: "Unto Him that loved us, and washed us from our sins in His own blood, And hath made us kings and priests unto God and His Father; to Him be glory and dominion for ever and ever. Amen" (Revelation 1:5-6).

b. *A Moral Cleansing.* "And Aaron and his sons thou shalt . . . wash . . . with water" (Exodus 29:4). There is an initial washing of regeneration which Paul refers to in Titus 3:5: "Not by works of righteousness which we have done, but according to His mercy He saved us, by the washing of regeneration, and renewing of the Holy Ghost." And there is also the continual cleansing by the Word, by which we are daily sanctified. We are told: "Christ . . . loved the church, and gave Himself for it; That He might sanctify and cleanse it with the washing of water by the word" (Ephesians 5:25-26).

As we have seen already in these studies, no sacrifice could be offered or service performed without washing at the laver. So we see that the priests had to be called and cleansed and then:

3. Clothed

"And for Aaron's sons thou shalt make coats, and thou

shalt make for them girdles, and bonnets shalt thou make for them, for glory and for beauty. . . . And thou shalt make them linen breeches to cover their nakedness; from the loins even unto the thighs they shall reach" (Exodus 28:40,42). Aaron's special garments are not mentioned in this connection, since he is seen here as representing the priestly family. So the articles of apparel are restricted to:

a. *Coats* (Exodus 28:40). These speak of *salvation.* "He hath clothed me with the garments of salvation, He hath covered me with the robe of righteousness" (Isaiah 61:10). These coats remind us of the coats of skin which God made for our first parents (Genesis 3:21). Only thus clad can we stand before a holy God.

b. *Girdles.* These speak of *service.* Our Lord's words to us are: "Let your loins be girded about, and your lights burning; And ye yourselves like unto men that wait for their lord" (Luke 12:35-36). Oh, to be characterized by such preparedness for worship and witness!

c. *The Bonnets.* These speak of *subjection.* "The head of every man is Christ; and the head of the woman is the man" (1 Corinthians 11:3). God would have us as obedient children, not doing our own will or seeking our own pleasure; but bringing every thought, word, and act into subjection to the obedience of Christ.

d. *The Breeches* speak of *self-effacement.* They were to cover the nakedness, from the loins even unto the thighs (Exodus 28:42). When Aaron is viewed alone, the breeches are not mentioned; but when he is associated with his sons, it appears that he also had to wear them.

David tells us that the Lord "taketh not pleasure in the legs of a man" (Psalm 147:10). The New Testament reminds us that we must "put . . . on the Lord Jesus Christ, and make not provision for the flesh, to fulfil the lusts thereof" (Romans 13:14). So if we would serve as acceptable priests, we must have a genuine experience of salvation, service, and self-effacement in the power of Christ our Great High Priest.

4. Consecrated

"Thou shalt consecrate Aaron and his sons" (Exodus 29:9). The solemn and sacred ceremony that effected this consecration is detailed for us in verses 10-36. It involved:

a. *Personal Dedication.* "Thou shalt also take one ram; and Aaron and his sons shall put their hands upon the head of the ram. . . . And thou shalt burn the whole ram upon the altar: it is a burnt offering unto the LORD" (Exodus 29:15,18). Before we can serve God acceptably as priests, we must know what it is to yield our bodies "a living sacrifice, holy, acceptable unto God, which is [our] reasonable service" (Romans 12:1). Nothing less than the dedication of our total faculties constitutes a "whole ram upon the altar."

b. *Moral Separation.* "Thou shalt take the other ram; and Aaron and his sons shall put their hands upon the head of the ram. Then shalt thou kill the ram, and take of his blood, and put it upon the tip of the right ear of Aaron, and upon the tip of the right ear of his sons, and upon the thumb of their right hand, and upon the great toe of their right foot, and sprinkle the blood upon the altar round about. And thou shalt take of the blood that is upon the altar, and of the anointing oil, and sprinkle it upon Aaron, and upon his garments, and upon his sons, and upon the garments of his sons with him: and he shall be hallowed" (Exodus 29:19-21). These verses teach that moral separation means:

1) *Separation from Sin.* The blood, applied to the right ear, right thumb, and right toe, demands a life of holiness. As those separated, we cannot tolerate sin in word, work, or walk. John tells us: "If we walk in the light, as He is in the light, we have fellowship one with another, and the blood of Jesus Christ His Son cleanseth us from all sin" (1 John 1:7).

2) *Separation unto Service.* The blood from the altar and

the anointing oil were sprinkled on the garments of Aaron and his sons. The garments spoke of their office and ministry; and therefore, when identified with the blood and oil, indicated complete separation unto the service of God.

Speaking of believers, Paul could say: "Ye are washed . . . ye are sanctified . . . ye are justified in the name of the Lord Jesus, and by the Spirit of our God" (1 Corinthians 6:11). Only thus could they be qualified to worship and serve in the assembly of God.

c. *Spiritual Realization.* "Thou shalt take of the ram . . . and one loaf of bread, and one cake of oiled bread, and one wafer . . . and thou shalt put all in the hands of Aaron, and in the hands of his sons; and shalt wave them for a wave offering before the LORD . . . and thou shalt take the ram of the consecration, and seethe his flesh in the holy place. And Aaron and his sons shall eat the flesh of the ram" (Exodus 29:22,23,24,31,32).

Consecration is not complete unless it leads to a realization of the preciousness of Christ to God, as well as the preciousness of Christ to the soul.

The priests were to take the most sacred parts of the ram of consecration and hold them out toward all quarters of the sky to signify the presentation of that which was most precious to God. These parts were then offered upon the altar in sacrifice. Later, the other parts of the ram were to be eaten by Aaron and his sons. Nothing was to be wasted or carried over to the next day. In this way the priests were made to realize the spiritual significance of their own consecration and commission.

When we come to the New Testament, we find that after Paul has besought his readers at Rome to yield themselves completely to God, and has warned them about being conformed to the world, he proceeds to say: "ye [shall know] what is that good, and acceptable, and perfect will of God"

(Romans 12:1-2). In other words, consecration involves personal dedication, moral separation, and spiritual realization.

So we have seen what constitutes the call, cleansing, clothing, and consecration of the priests. Oh, that this should be our experience within the local church of God!

### III. AARON AND THE LEVITES

The Levites were the priestly family, and their history is interesting to study. What is relevant in this particular context is that they constituted part of the priesthood, and to them were committed certain responsibilities in the charge of the Tabernacle. Before they were fit to serve under the supervision of Aaron and his family, they had to be:

1. Purified

"And the LORD spake unto Moses, saying, Take the Levites from among the children of Israel, and cleanse them" (Numbers 8:5-6). In the verses that follow, that is 6-15, we see how judicially and morally they underwent a solemn ceremony of cleansing. We have seen already how necessary this is for any of us who serve corporately as priests, but it is just as necessary if we serve as individuals. The Word tells us: "Be ye clean, that bear the vessels of the LORD" (Isaiah 52:11).

2. Mobilized

"And the LORD spake unto Moses . . . saying, Number the children of Levi after the house of their fathers, by their families: every male from a month old and upward shalt thou number them" (Numbers 3:14-15). Every available male was registered for service in connection with the Tabernacle. This teaches us the thrilling yet solemn fact that God expects every Christian to be occupied in some specific service for Him. Paul tells us that "we are . . . created in Christ Jesus unto good works, which God hath before ordained that we should walk in them" (Ephesians 2:10).

Not only were the Levites numbered, but they were *positioned,* as is clear from Numbers 3:23,29,35. They flanked the Tabernacle so as to guard it and serve it.

3. Utilized

The word concerning them was that they "shall minister with their brethren in the tabernacle of the congregation, to keep the charge, and shall do no service" (or, no other service, Numbers 8:26). In Numbers 3:25-26 we have listed the various duties that were delegated to each family in the tribe of Levi. The Gershonites had charge of the curtains; the Kohathites carried the holy vessels; and Merarites were entrusted with the boards, pillars, pins, and cords. A Merarite carrying a tiny pin, or taking charge of a seemingly insignificant cord, was doing God's service as much as the Kohathite who carried the ark or the mercy seat. So today, God has set the members "every one . . . in the body, as it hath pleased Him," and the Holy Spirit has divided the various gifts "to every man severally as He will" (1 Corinthians 12:18,11).

Thus we have seen what constitutes the priesthood of the Tabernacle. In Aaron we see the priesthood pre-eminently; in Aaron and his sons we view the priesthood universally; and in Aaron and the Levites we view the priesthood individually. God enable us to understand our privileges as priests unto Him, and to draw heavily upon the resources that are available for us in our Great High Priest, even our Lord Jesus Christ.

# Chapter 10

## THE OFFERINGS

### *Scriptures for Study*

Then a cloud covered the tent of the congregation, and the glory of the LORD filled the tabernacle. And Moses was not able to enter into the tent of the congregation, because the cloud abode thereon, and the glory of the LORD filled the tabernacle. And when the cloud was taken up from over the tabernacle, the children of Israel went onward in all their journeys: But if the cloud were not taken up, then they journeyed not till the day that it was taken up. For the cloud of the LORD was upon the tabernacle by day, and fire was on it by night, in the sight of all the house of Israel, throughout all their journeys (Exodus 40:34-38).

And the LORD called unto Moses, and spake unto him out of the tabernacle of the congregation, saying, Speak unto the children of Israel, and say unto them, If any man of you bring an offering unto the LORD, ye shall bring your offering of the cattle, even of the herd, and of the flock. If his offering be a burnt sacrifice of the herd, let him offer a male without blemish: he shall offer it of his own voluntary will at the door of the tabernacle of the congregation before the LORD. And he shall put his hand upon the head of the burnt offering; and it shall be accepted for him to make atonement for him. And he shall kill the bullock before the LORD: and the priests, Aaron's sons, shall bring the blood, and sprinkle the blood round about upon the altar that is by the door of the tabernacle of the congregation. And he shall flay the burnt offering, and cut it into his pieces. And the sons of Aaron the priest shall put fire upon the altar, and lay the wood in order upon the fire: And the priests, Aaron's sons, shall lay the parts, the head, and the fat, in order upon the wood that is on the fire which is upon the altar: But his inwards and his legs shall he wash in water: and the priest shall burn all on the altar, to be a burnt sacrifice, an offering made by fire, of a sweet savour unto the LORD.

And if his offering be of the flocks, namely, of the sheep, or of the goats, for a burnt sacrifice; he shall bring it a male without blemish. And he shall kill it on the side of the altar northward before the LORD: and the priests, Aaron's sons, shall sprinkle his blood round about upon the altar. And he shall cut it into his pieces, with his head and his fat: and the priest shall lay them in order on the wood that is on the fire which is upon the altar: But he shall wash the inwards and the legs with water: and the priest shall bring it all, and burn it upon the altar: it is a burnt sacrifice, an offering made by fire, of a sweet savour unto the LORD.

And if the burnt sacrifice for his offering to the LORD be of fowls, then he shall bring his offering of turtledoves, or of young pigeons. And the priest shall bring it unto the altar, and wring off his head, and burn it on the altar; and the blood thereof shall be wrung out at the side of the altar: And he shall pluck away his crop with his feathers, and cast it beside the altar on the east part, by the place of the ashes: And he shall cleave it with the wings thereof, but shall not divide it asunder: and the priest shall burn it upon the altar, upon the wood that is upon the fire: it is a burnt sacrifice, an offering made by fire, of a sweet savour unto the LORD (Leviticus 1:1-17; see also Leviticus 13—14; 16—17; Numbers 19; Hebrews 7—10).


## THE OFFERINGS

Scriptures for Study: Exodus 40:34-38; Leviticus 1:1-17; 13—14; 16—17; Numbers 19; Hebrews 7—10

# I. THE DEDICATORY OFFERINGS

1. The Burnt Offering

2. The Meal Offering

3. The Peace Offering

# II. THE EXPIATORY OFFERINGS

1. The Sin Offering
    a. The Skin — the winsomeness of sin
    b. The Flesh — the wantonness of sin
    c. The Head — the willfulness of sin
    d. The Legs — the waywardness of sin
    e. The Inwards — the wickedness of sin
    f. The Dung — the wastefulness of sin

2. The Trespass Offering

# III. THE COMPLEMENTARY OFFERINGS

1. The Problem of Disease

2. The Problem of Defilement

So far we have given attention to the Tabernacle, its furniture, and its priesthood. The one important consideration which remains is that of the offerings. This is a vast subject, full of rich teaching, so we cannot do more than introduce it and hope that the outline given will encourage a closer examination.

You will have observed that, up until now, all the instructions given concerning the Tabernacle were communicated to

Moses in the mount; but when it comes to the offerings, the divine directions are spoken to him out of the Tabernacle. In the closing chapter of Exodus we read: "Then a cloud covered the tent of the congregation, and the glory of the LORD filled the tabernacle" (Exodus 40:34).

God's tent of meeting was now complete and the priesthood established. Worship and witness were about to commence. So we read in the first verse of the first chapter of Leviticus: "And the LORD called unto Moses, and spake unto him out of the tabernacle of the congregation, saying, Speak unto the children of Israel, and say unto them, If any man of you bring an offering unto the LORD, ye shall bring your offering of the cattle, even of the herd, and of the flock." It was from within the Tabernacle that the Lord spoke, and not from Mount Sinai. His glory having filled the Tabernacle, God now revealed Himself through the sacrifices that were designed to fit the sinner to dwell in that divine glory.

If we turn to Hebrews we read that "every high priest taken from among men is ordained for men in things pertaining to God, that he may offer both gifts and sacrifices for sins" (5:1). Here we have set before us the two main categories of offerings which were presented to God. They are called *gifts* and *sacrifices.* One stands for dedicatory offerings, while the other for expiatory offerings. This division is a key to the first seven chapters of Leviticus, for there we find five offerings mentioned: the first three being dedicatory, and the last two expiatory. A complete study of the offerings, however, reveals that there are more than five in the divine instructions, and these might well be termed complementary offerings. Among these we shall concern ourselves with the cleansing of the leper (Leviticus 13—14) and the provision for wilderness defilement (Numbers 19).

In our consideration of all these offerings, it is well to

bear in mind the words of Henry Batchelor, when he says that the Levitical offerings were "presented by men *in* the favor of God, and by men *out* of the favor of God. If a man had broken revealed laws he was out of favor and the sin offering or trespass offering was the means of restoring him to favor. The man who had broken no law brought a burnt offering or a peace offering at the dictate of voluntary piety. The sin or trespass offering acknowledged that the worshiper was out of favor, and was brought in accordance with explicit requirements. The burnt offering or peace offering, on the contrary, was the spontaneous service of one in the divine favor."

Let us, then, consider the offerings in terms of their threefold division:

## I. THE DEDICATORY OFFERINGS

These were three in number and foreshadowed the *value* of Christ's death. They are called the burnt offering, the meal offering, and the peace offering. Though each has atonement value, their main intention was to prefigure Christ as a "sweetsmelling savour" to God, rather than as a sin offering.

1. The Burnt Offering (Leviticus 1; 6:8-13; Hebrews 10:7-8)

The burnt offering speaks of the value of the death of Christ, in terms of His *devotion.* The Hebrew word translated *burnt* offering signifies "that which goes up" or "ascends." It was a voluntary offering, wholly consumed on the brazen altar.

This offering could be taken from the *herd* (Leviticus 1:3-9) — a bullock without blemish; from the *flock* (Leviticus 1:10-12) — a sheep or a goat without blemish; or from the *birds* (Leviticus 1:14-17) — turtledoves or young pigeons without blemish.

The *bullock,* or ox, typifies devoted service. In the divine instructions concerning animals, God says: "Thou shalt not muzzle the ox when he treadeth out the corn" (Deuteronomy 25:4). The bullock plowed the land, brought home the sheaves from the harvest field, trod out the corn for the household, and so in every sense typifies willing service.

The *sheep* typifies devoted submission. Isaiah reminds us that when the Lord Jesus was led out to Calvary, He was brought "as a lamb to the slaughter, and as a sheep before her shearers is dumb, so He opened not His mouth" (Isaiah 53:7).

The *goat* typifies sin-bearing. On the Day of Atonement the scapegoat, or live goat, was brought to the door of the Tabernacle, and Aaron was to lay both his hands on his head and "confess over him all the iniquities of the children of Israel, and all their transgressions in all their sins, putting them upon the head of the goat, and shall send him away by the hand of a fit man into the wilderness." The record continues: "And the goat shall bear upon him all their iniquities unto a land not inhabited" (Leviticus 16:21-22).

The *turtledoves,* or young pigeons, typify devoted sacrifice. When an offerer brought doves or pigeons, it was because he could afford nothing more. At the dedication of Jesus, Mary and Joseph offered "a sacrifice according to that which is said in the law of the Lord, A pair of turtledoves, or two young pigeons" (Luke 2:24).

So we see that each kind of sacrifice carries its own significance and represents a different aspect of the Person and work of Christ. With the apostle we can say: "Christ also hath loved us, and hath given Himself for us an offering and a sacrifice to God for a sweetsmelling savour" (Ephesians 5:2).

In the burnt offering the merit of the sacrifice was transferred in type to the offerer so that he stood in all the acceptance of the offering before a holy God. This teaches us that our only acceptance before God, as we bring ourselves in sacrifice, is the merit and value of Christ's burnt offering for us.

After identifying himself with his sacrifice, the offerer was to slay his own bullock, sheep, goat, or bird; then solemnly watch the priest as he sprinkled the blood in God's prescribed manner, and lay the sacrifice in its several parts upon the altar. All this would impress upon the offerer the solemnity and reality of true yieldedness and devotedness to God. Without doubt, the Apostle Paul had in mind the burnt offering, when he said: "I beseech you therefore, brethren, by the mercies of God, that ye present your bodies a living sacrifice, holy, acceptable unto God, which is your reasonable service" (Romans 12:1).

2. The Meal Offering (Leviticus 2; 6:14-23; Hebrews 7:27)

The meal (or meat) offering speaks of the value of the death of Christ in terms of its *perfection.* It was composed of fine flour or green ears of corn, with frankincense, oil, and salt (Leviticus 2:1-16).

The *fine flour, or green ears of corn,* typify the perfect humanity of our Lord Jesus Christ. They are the product of the earth and refer to the kinship of Christ with man. He was "made like unto His brethren" (Hebrews 2:17). The flour speaks of the perfect evenness of His life, while the green corn suggests the youthfulness of His life. He was "holy, harmless, undefiled, separate from sinners" (Hebrews 7:26). In the words of prophecy, He could say: "I said, O My God, take Me not away in the midst of My days" (Psalm 102:24).

In the *oil* of mingling and the oil of anointing we see the holiness of His life, as One indwelt and anointed by the Holy Spirit. Paul tells us that Jesus Christ was "declared to be the Son of God with power, according to the spirit of holiness" (Romans 1:4).

The *frankincense* refers to His graciousness, for everything He did or said went up to God as "a sacrifice . . . for a sweetsmelling savour" (Ephesians 5:2). The common people said: "He hath done all things well" (Mark 7:37). Those who heard Him "wondered at the gracious words which proceeded out of His mouth" (Luke 4:22).

The *salt* refers to the faithfulness of His life. "Every oblation of thy meal offering shalt thou season with salt; neither shalt thou suffer the salt of the covenant of thy God to be lacking from thy meal offering: with all thine offerings thou shalt offer salt" (Leviticus 2:13). Salt has a pungent, preserving influence. It is opposed to corruption, and as such symbolizes the faithfulness and truthfulness of our Lord Jesus, both in life and in word.

So we see something of the perfection of our Lord Jesus Christ, in terms of the evenness, youthfulness, holiness, graciousness, and faithfulness of His life.

In answer to those who say that the meal offering does not include the Lord's death, I would quote Ada R. Habershon's words: "It is true there is no mention of blood, but Leviticus 2:14 speaks of the 'firstfruits' as a meal offering. This is a type of His resurrection (Leviticus 23:10-11; 1 Corinthians 15:23). It seems evident that there must be some reference to His death earlier in the chapter. This is found in verse 6 (Leviticus 2): they were to 'part . . . in pieces' the loaf or cake, a type of broken bread (1 Corinthians 11:23-24). Also the word for cakes in verse 4 implies 'pierced cakes' (Newberry), and the action of fire (baking, etc.) suggests judgment."

As a matter of fact, the threefold way in which the meal offering could be treated speaks eloquently of the Saviour's sufferings. The meal offering could be baked on a flat plate (Leviticus 2:5). The word "pan" there should be "flat plate." This speaks of Christ's sufferings in His body. They were open to public view. He could say: "They pierced My hands and My feet. I . . . tell all My bones: they look and stare upon Me" (Psalm 22:16-17). The meal offering could be baked in a frying pan (Leviticus 2:7). The word "fryingpan" is more accurately "pan," signifying a vessel deeper than a frying pan, used for boiling food as well as baking it. This speaks of Christ's sufferings in His soul. These were partially understood by those who witnessed something of His agony in Gethsemane, when He said, "My soul is exceeding sorrowful, even unto death" (Matthew 26:38). The meal offering could be baked in the oven (Leviticus 2:4). The oven was a vessel of earthenware, heated by a fire in the inside. This speaks of Christ's sufferings in His spirit. So mysterious and awesome is this realm of suffering that God hid His Son in darkness while He "made Him to be sin for us, who knew no sin" (2 Corinthians 5:21). It was in that hour that He gave expression to that cry of dereliction, "My God, My God, why hast Thou forsaken Me?" (Psalm 22:1)

So in the meal offering we see the value of Christ's death in terms of its perfection. He was, and is, the perfect Saviour.

3. The Peace Offering

This speaks of the value of the death of Christ in terms of His *communion* (Leviticus 3; 7:11-13; Romans 5:1; Colossians 1:20). This was not an offering to make peace, but rather an offering that celebrated and rejoiced in the peace already made. As someone has said: "It is the offering which typifies to us the communion of saints." When referring to the precious blood, which is symbolized in the wine, Paul says: "The cup of blessing which we bless, is it not the communion of the blood of Christ?" Again: "The bread which we break, is it not the communion of the body of Christ?" (1 Corinthians 10:16)

The animals used for sacrifice in the peace offering were the same as those employed in the burnt offering, except that the female as well as the male of the herd and of the flock was admissible. Also, turtledoves and young pigeons were not to be used. The poor who could not afford a bullock, a sheep, or a goat, could always share in the rich man's offering: hence, the exclusion of the birds. In our fellowship with God and with one another, there is neither male nor female. So Paul reminds us that by virtue of our baptism into Christ, and therefore union with Christ, we are "all one in Christ Jesus" (Galatians 3:28).

In addition to the instructions concerning identification, the slaying of the victim, and the sprinkling of the blood, God commanded the priests to present to Him the breast as a wave offering before the Lord (Leviticus 7:30); and to retain and eat the shoulder as a heave offering. This is highly significant, for in our appreciation of the Lord Jesus in communion, that which speaks of affection and love is offered up to God in worship, while we, as priests, share in the heave shoulder, which speaks of strength.

A solemn warning accompanied the way in which the flesh was to be eaten: "It shall be eaten the same day ye offer it, and on the morrow: and if ought remain until the third day, it shall be burnt in the fire. And if it be eaten at all on the third day, it is abominable; it shall not be accepted. Therefore every one that eateth it shall bear his iniquity, because he hath profaned the hallowed thing of the Lord: and that soul shall be cut off from among his people" (Leviticus 19:6-8).

What solemn teaching this is! God insists that our experience of communion in the Lord Jesus should be fresh and real. To become stale in our appreciation of our Lord Jesus Christ is to be cut off from fellowship. This applies not only to our quiet times, but to the holy celebration when we come together for the remembrance of the Lord in His death, until He come.

Thus we have seen something of the value of the death of

Christ to God and to His believing people, in terms of the Saviour's devotion, perfection, and communion.

Now we turn to the next category of offerings:


## II. THE EXPIATORY OFFERINGS

These were two in number, and foreshadowed the *victory* of Christ's death. They are called the sin offering and the trespass offering and are essentially atoning sacrifices to deal with sin and the sinner.

1. The Sin Offering (Leviticus 4; 6:24-30; 2 Corinthians 5:21)

The sin offering speaks of the death of Christ in terms of its victory over sin. The animals involved in this sacrifice were male and female, of the herd and of the flock, of turtledoves and young pigeons, or the tenth ephah of flour.

Furthermore, God specified that a sin offering had to vary in terms of:

> The sin of the anointed priest (Leviticus 4:3-12)
>
> The sin of the whole congregation (Leviticus 4:13-21)
>
> The sin of the ruler (Leviticus 4:22-26)
>
> The sin of the individual (Leviticus 4:27-35)

After the identification with the offerer and the application of the blood, all sin offerings were taken outside the camp, any distance up to six miles, and wholly burned.

The New Testament commentary on this reads: "For the bodies of those beasts, whose blood is brought into the sanctuary by the high priest for sin, are burned without the camp. Wherefore Jesus also, that He might sanctify the people with His own blood, suffered without the gate" (Hebrews 13:11-12). Not only did He endure separation from the city, but separation from God in order that He might be "made . . . sin for us, who knew no sin; that we might be made the righteousness of God in Him" (2 Corinthians 5:21).

To show the seriousness of sin, and the severity of divine judgment upon it, God enumerated the various parts of the animal that had to be burned (Leviticus 4:11).

a. *The Skin* speaks of the winsomeness of sin; for let us never forget that there are "pleasures of sin" (Hebrews 11:25), and just as the skin of the bullock was its most attractive part, so sin has a certain winsomeness.

b. *The Flesh* speaks of the wantonness of sin. Paul tells us that "the works of the flesh are manifest, which are these; adultery, fornication, uncleanness, lasciviousness, idolatry, witchcraft, hatred, variance, emulations, wrath, strife, seditions, heresies" (Galatians 5:19-20).

c. *The Head* speaks of the willfulness of sin. God looks upon man and sees that "every imagination of the thoughts of his heart [is] only evil continually" (Genesis 6:5).

d. *The Legs* speak of the waywardness of sin. "All we like sheep have gone astray; we have turned every one to his own way; and the LORD hath laid on Him the iniquity of us all" (Isaiah 53:6).

e. *The Inwards* speak of the wickedness of sin. "The heart is deceitful above all things, and desperately wicked" (Jeremiah 17:9).

f. *The Dung* speaks of the wastefulness of sin. James tell us: "When lust hath conceived, it bringeth forth sin: and sin, when it is finished, bringeth forth death" (1:15).

Now in the sin offering every aspect of sin had to come under God's severest judgment. So we learn that God has no half measures with sin. He has dealt with it in its totality and with finality.

Within the scope of the sin offerings must be included the *great Day of Atonement,* detailed for us with all its impressive ritual in Leviticus 16. On that day, however, only the high priest, garbed in his linen coat, was allowed to officiate (speaking of Christ, who humbled Himself even unto death). The two aspects of the atonement, namely propitiation and substitution, are vividly foreshadowed in the sacrifices offered. Having atoned for himself, his sons, and the tabernacle, the high priest then turned his attention to the whole nation.

*Propitiation* was represented in the slain goat, whose blood was taken into the holiest of all and sprinkled once on the mercy seat and seven times before it. One application of blood suffices God, but it takes seven to convince man of its preciousness and efficacy.

The live goat represented *substitution.* It was identified with the blood of the slain one, was made the sin-bearer for the whole nation, and led away into a place uninhabited (Leviticus 16:9-10). How wonderful to know that, "As far as the east is from the west, so far hath He removed our transgressions from us" (Psalm 103:12). Again: "Thou wilt cast all their sins into the depths of the sea" (Micah 7:19). Once again: "Thou hast cast all my sins behind Thy back" (Isaiah 38:17). Then the New Testament word: "[Your] sins and iniquities will I remember no more" (Hebrews 10:17).

How our hearts should well up in praise for "the Lamb of God, which [beareth] away the sin of the world" (John 1:29!)

2. The Trespass Offering

This speaks of the death of Christ in terms of its victory over the sinner. In the sin offering the emphasis is on the principle of sin, while the trespass offering has in view the practice of sin. The sacrifices used for the trespass offering were the same as those employed in the sin offering. A tenth ephah of flour represented the sacrifices of the poorest of the poor. It has been pointed out that it was flour, not grain, representing that which has been produced through grinding or pounding, and therefore symbolizing that which comes out of suffering.

The trespass offering covered every transgression, save a sin unto death. A twofold condition accompanied the presentation of a trespass offering. The first was *confession* of the sin committed: "He shall confess that he hath sinned in that thing" (Leviticus 5:5). "That thing" implies that the confession had to relate to particular things (1 John 1:9). The second was *compensation:* "He shall make amends for the harm that he hath done . . . and shall add the fifth part thereto" (Leviticus 5:16). Too little is taught in our day of the doctrine of restitution. Without it, however, there can be no reality of repentance and faith, which are the grounds of cleansing and forgiveness (Ephesians 4:28).

Thank God, in the trespass offering we see the divine provision that has been made for any break in fellowship with Him. So John tells us: "If we confess our sins, He is faithful and just to forgive us our sins, and to cleanse us from all unrighteousness" (1 John 1:9). To live in the good of this continual cleansing and forgiveness is to know victory in our daily life. For this we have that glorious assurance of the Apostle Paul: "sin shall not have dominion over you: for ye are not under the law, but under grace" (Romans 6:14).

In the sin offering and trespass offering we have the foreshadowing of God's provision for victory over the principle and practice of sin in our lives. How great is the salvation that we have through our Lord Jesus Christ!

### III. THE COMPLEMENTARY OFFERINGS

These were two in number and foreshadowed the *virtue* of Christ's death. They were offerings designed to deal with the problems of disease and defilement.

1. The Problem of Disease (Leviticus 13 and 14)

Leprosy is a symbol of the direct effect of sin. We notice

that the plague affected the person, the garments, and the house of those afflicted. The uncleanness of leprosy demanded judgment. "The priest shall pronounce him utterly unclean" (Leviticus 13:44). This, in turn, issued in separation: "He shall dwell alone; without the camp shall his habitation be" (Leviticus 13:46).

Despite its utter loathsomeness and incurableness, God made provision for its cleansing. Through God's representative priest, the leper was commanded to take two birds (Leviticus 14:4). One was slain in an earthen vessel over running water, suggestive of our Lord in His humanity, offering Himself through the eternal Spirit without spot unto God (see Hebrews 10:5; 9:14). The living bird, together with the cedar wood, scarlet, and hyssop, was identified with the slain bird, inasmuch as it was dipped in the blood. The cedar wood, scarlet, and hyssop intensify the thought of Christ's sufferings by typifying the glory of the cross, the death of the cross, and the shame of the cross. The living bird was then let loose into the open field and allowed to fly into the heavens.

How wonderfully this sets forth our blessed Lord, who was "delivered for our offences, and . . . raised again for our justification" (Romans 4:25)! Just as the bird with blood-marked wings flew up to the heavens, so we learn that Christ, "Neither by the blood of goats and calves, but by His own blood . . . entered in once into the holy place, having obtained eternal redemption for us" (Hebrews 9:12).

Through the merits of this sacrifice, the leper was judicially cleansed by the sprinkling of the blood. "He shall sprinkle upon him that is to be cleansed from the leprosy seven times, and shall pronounce him clean" (Leviticus 14:7). And he was morally cleansed by the washing of water. "He that is to be cleansed shall wash his clothes, and shave off all his hair, and wash himself in water, that he may be clean"

(Leviticus 14:8). After that there was restoration: "he shall come into the camp" (Leviticus 14:8); and then consecration. The blood and the oil were applied to the ear, hand, and foot, as in the consecration of the priests.

This cleansing of the leper teaches us how God can deal radically with the effects of sin in a man's life. The disease of sin eats deeply into some people's lives; but thank God, the cross of Christ is more than adequate for this condition.

2. The Problem of Defilement (Numbers 19)

If leprosy signifies the disease of sin, then a dead body represents the defilement of sin. Such defilement can lead to a state of backsliding. So we find God making provision for this problem of defilement.

It is interesting to note from the context that this divine provision followed the rebellion of Korah and his sons. There was a pollution that could be dealt with through the trespass offering, but uncleanness resulting from rebellion required extraordinary means. So God commanded Eleazar the priest to take a red heifer outside the camp and slay it, and then burn it with appropriate ceremonies to remove the uncleanness from the people. The "red heifer without spot" (Numbers 19:2) speaks, of course, of the Lord Jesus who "offered Himself without spot to God" (Hebrews 9:14). Suffering outside the camp shows God's view of the heinousness of sin; but, having dealt with it adequately, there is now a permanent provision for cleansing and restoration.

For the children of Israel, the offering of the red heifer was to be "a statute for ever" (Numbers 19:10). Anyone who touched a dead body should be unclean seven days. On the third day he was to be sprinkled with water containing the ashes of the burnt heifer, and on the seventh day he was to wash and be clean. This teaches us that when a Christian defiles his conscience by dead things, that is to say, things of the past old life in the world, he is cut off from fellowship with God and is in a state of backsliding. The Scriptures teach that he need not to be converted again; Christ cannot die again. The blood on the mercy seat still speaks of perfect remission (Hebrews 10:18), but he needs the application of ashes and the water of separation. Ashes speak of the remembrance of Calvary, while the water signifies the Word of God applied in the power of the Spirit of God, correcting the wrong thing and separating the believer afresh unto God. So Paul exhorts his readers at Corinth to "cleanse [themselves] from all filthiness of the flesh and spirit" (2 Corinthians 7:1).

The value and meaning of this offering is directly referred to in Hebrews 9:13-14: "If the blood of bulls and of goats, and the ashes of an heifer sprinkling the unclean, sanctifieth to the purifying of the flesh: How much more shall the blood of Christ, who through the eternal Spirit offered Himself without spot to God, purge your conscience from dead works to serve the living God?" How wonderfully this illustrates the unity and reality of progressive teaching throughout the Bible. The red heifer of the Old Testament is the matchless Saviour of the New, whose virtuous death not only deals with the disease of sin, but also the defilement of sin.

Thus we have considered the Tabernacle with its offerings. We have merely touched the fringe of the detailed and rich teaching of the shadows and types. It is sincerely hoped, however, that even with this outline something of the sweep, power, and glory of Christ's redemptive work, in all its preciousness Godward, and effectiveness manward, will have been conveyed to each one of us. In the dedicatory offerings we see in Christ perfect satisfaction for God, while in the expiatory and complementary offerings we see in Christ perfect salvation for man. With such a view of the Christ of Calvary we cannot but say, "Hallelujah, what a Saviour!"

# APPENDIX

Studies on the Tabernacle would be incomplete without a reference to the recent and intriguing work of Meir Ben Uri. Writing in *Christianity Today* ("Tabernacle Furnishings — Recreating the Divine Design,"* March 12, 1971), Dwight L. Baker informs us that Meir Ben Uri, aged 62 years, is "Israel's foremost religious artist and synagogue designer," who "feels that the illustrations commonly used are based upon sketches drawn during the Middle Ages to catch the eyes of children. They bear scant resemblance, he says, to the actual objects the ancient Hebrews carted around the desert.

"A painstaking scholar and a devout, Orthodox Jew, Ben Uri set out to correct the misimpressions. After three years of work he came up with replicas of the golden altar and priests' laver (see illustrations). He regards these as accurate models based upon specifications given to Moses by God. . . . He says: 'I have profound belief in the literal correctness of the Hebrew text and as given, I might reconstruct the entire Tabernacle and all of its holy furniture.'

"To Ben Uri, such work is much more than mere sentiment for antiquity. He feels that ancient Israel has a unique message to other nations through architecture. Affirming a theological dimension in architecture, he contends that 'to build without divine mandate is to create disorder. Much of the sickness and chaos of today's megalopolis is a direct result of "unauthorized" architecture.'

"Ben Uri stresses simplicity and small structures. He estimates that Solomon's Temple could be built today for the relatively small sum of $1 million. 'To build a tabernacle is a primitive thing,' he says. 'We are

*Copyright 1971 by *Christianity Today*; reprinted by permission.

181

in great need today to rediscover this simplicity. In our world God wants us to have *Shkenah* (the divine presence), but instead we have *shkunah* (tenement house).'

"A few weeks ago Ben Uri was called to the home of Israel's president, Zalman Shazar, to talk about his model of the golden altar. Shazar, who is said to follow the progress of Ben Uri's studies, spent forty minutes with the architect.

"In recreating the Tabernacle furnishings, Ben Uri kept in mind that Moses was well educated in Egyptian architecture. He also tried to forget the popular embellishments of artists strongly influenced by Byzantine models and ideas. But most important, he tried to follow meticulously the instructions given in Scripture. He contends that through a system of Hebrew letter and word values, any object that God commanded to be built can be reconstructed.

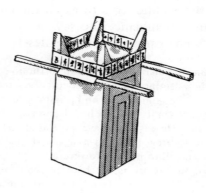

Golden altar

"For the altar, Ben Uri used the 56 Hebrew words and 236 letters in God's instructions to Moses (Exodus 37:25-28). In the process he believes he corrected an error in translation concerning the way the altar was fitted to be transported. Contrary to the interpretation that poles were slipped through two rings on opposite corners, Ben Uri says they passed through square housings. (He translates the Hebrew *batim* as 'housings' rather than 'rings.') These housings, he declares, made for better balance and resemble those on Egyptian chair thrones.

Bronze laver

"For the bronze laver, Ben Uri used the 49 Hebrew words and their 225 component letters in the three sentences of the Exodus text (30:18,28). His design also was benefitted by his extensive study of ancient water installations and fittings (the Tabernacle laver was used for purification rites). Its footing consists of two large triangles that suspend a rod attached to the water bowl. As the priest tipped the laver, a stream of water would emerge from a spout. The laver has previously been pictured with four sturdy legs supporting a basin fitted with valve-type spigots, which, according to Ben Uri, did not exist 3,000 years ago."

Students of the Tabernacle will want to examine Ben Uri's writings and designs for further light on the structure and furniture of God's "tent of testimony" in the wilderness. The fact that his sketches bear "scant resemblance" to the illustrations commonly accepted by Bible scholars throughout the centuries must not disturb us unduly. On the contrary, these "theological dimensions in architecture" can only serve to sharpen our understanding and, therefore, our application of the essential message of the Tabernacle, which is *camping with God.*

# BIBLIOGRAPHY

Atwater, Edward E. *The Sacred Tabernacle of the Hebrews.* New York, Dodd, Mead & Co., 1875.

Caldecott, W. Shaw. *The Tabernacle: Its History and Structure.* 2nd ed. London, The Religious Tract Society, 1906.

Darby, J. N. *Hints on the Tabernacle, etc.* London, G. Morrish.

Davidson, I. E. *The Tabernacle.* Chislehurst, Kent, England, Barbican Book Room.

DeHaan, M. R. *The Tabernacle.* Grand Rapids, Zondervan Publishing House, 1955, p. 13.

Dorricott, J. *Meditations on the Tabernacle,* 1920.

Edersheim, A. E. *The Temple: Its Ministry and Service at the Time of Jesus Christ.* New ed. rev. Boston, Ira Bradley & Co., 1881.

Habershon, Ada R. *Outline Studies of the Tabernacle.* London, Marshall, Morgan & Scott, p. 20.

-----. *The Study of the Types.* Grand Rapids, Kregel Publications, 1961.

Haldeman, I. M. *The Tabernacle Priesthood and Offerings.* Old Tappan, New Jersey, Fleming H. Revell Co., 1925.

Hucklesby, George. *The Tabernacle of Old.* 2nd ed. rev. Glasgow, Pickering & Inglis.

Kingscote, R. F. *Christ as Seen in the Offerings.* London, G. Morrish.

Mackintosh, C. H. *Notes on the Book of Exodus.* Neptune, New Jersey, Loizeaux Brothers, Inc., 1959.

-----. *Notes on the Book of Leviticus.* Neptune, New Jersey, Loizeaux Brothers, Inc., 1959.

-----. *Notes on the Book of Numbers.* Neptune, New Jersey, Loizeaux Brothers, Inc., 1959.

Moorhead, W. G. *The Tabernacle (Studies in Mosaic Institutions).* Grand Rapids, Kregel Publications, 1957.

Mount, Jr., R. H. *The Law Prophesied.* Mansfield, Ohio, 1963.

Newberry, Thomas. *The Levitical Offerings.* Kilmarnock, Scotland, John Ritchie Ltd.

Pollock, A. J. *The Tabernacle's Typical Teaching.* London, The Central Bible Truth Depot.

Pont, Charles E. *Tabernacle Alphabet.* Neptune, New Jersey, Loizeaux Brothers, Inc., 1946.

Redwood, A. McDonald. *Jehovah's Trystings.* Bangalore, India, The Scripture Literature Depot, 1929.

-----. *Seven Old Testament Feasts.* London, Oliphants, Ltd.

Ridout, Samuel. *Lectures on the Tabernacle,* 6th ed. Neptune, New Jersey, Loizeaux Brothers, Inc., 1952.

Rodgers, George. *The Tabernacle and its Services.* London, Marshall, Morgan & Scott.

Sabiers, Karl G. *A Study of the Tabernacle.* Los Angeles, Robertson Publishing Co., 1944.

Scott, Walter. *The Tabernacle.* 2nd ed. Dedham, Essex, England, G. F. Vallance Ltd.

Simpson, A. B. *Christ in the Tabernacle.* Harrisburg, Pennsylvania, Christian Publications.

Slemming, C. W. *Made According to Pattern.* New and rev. London, Henry E. Walter Ltd., 1956, pp. 16, 17.

-----. *These are the Garments.* Fort Washington, Pennsylvania, Christian Literature Crusade, 1955.

Tatford, Fredk. A. *Tabernacle and Temple.* Kilmarnock, Scotland, John Ritchie Ltd.

Widdison, P. J. *Notes of Lectures on the Tabernacle.* Luton, Beds., England.

Yapp, Mrs. *Old Testament Shadows.* London, James E. Hawkins.